AutoFutropolis

What if Elvis had run Ford, vehicles could levitate, British Leyland had got their act together and other made up autoscenarios plus actual concept cars, some of which did shape the future.

Copyright © 2022 James Ruppert
www.foresightpublications.com
www.bangernomics.com
All rights reserved.
ISBN: 978-1-9160522-7-7
2022 Copyright © James Ruppert Also various images
Copyright motor manufacturers and available at the time of
publication for editorial use and with permission

James Ruppert

AutoFutropolis – car history rebooted

James Ruppert has asserted his moral right to be identified as the author of this work in accordance with the Copyright Designs and Patents Act 1988.

All rights reserved. No part of this publication may be reproduced, Stored in a retrieval system, or transmitted in any form or by any means electronic, mechanical, photocopying or otherwise without the prior permission of the copyright owner.

All images are copyright James Ruppert or motor manufacturers who supplied them for editorial use from motor shows, press releases, access to their photo archives, or via the Newspress service to professional journalists.

More information at www.bangernomics.com

www.foresightpublications.com

A CIP catalogue record for this book is available from the British Library

AutoFutropolis – car history rebooted

RetroDedication

To car designers who dared to think a bit differently. But mostly small boys who scribbled impossibly brilliant V28 supercharged flying car in their school textbooks instead of concentrating on their lessons. I hope they still do that, otherwise the future of car design is screwed.

Thanks Very Much for peering into an alternative future

Kelsey Publishing, Chris Hope who commissioned most of these and Paul Wager who gave permission for me to reproduce many of these stories that originally appeared in Classic Car Buyer, but . Thanks to Vauxhall and in particular Justin Hawkins for the main cover images and GKN, especially Kate Saxton and Chas Hallett for the Jensen FFF image. Finally, every single reader who buys my books, bothers to ask me questions, tell me off, show me what they have just bought and is generally really lovely and united by a love of all things motorised.

AutoFutropolis – Car History Rebooted

Contents

Autointroduction

1. E-Type spiked by the AC Dart 1

2. AMC Pacer, full steam ahead... 6

3. When Rolls Royce embraced the Black Knight 11

4. BMC Reborn: After Issigonis 15

5. Bricklin to the Future 20

6. Chrysler goes full Airflow 25

7. The Supersonic XJ 29

8. If Colin had Built Bungalows...34

9. That time De Tomaso won Le Mans 39

10. When Edsel became Elvis 44

11. Gamage Go Electric 49

12. Gilbern Made in Wales, still... 54

13. When Gordon Keeble saved Vauxhall from Europe 59

14. Billy Rootes and the Hillman Beetles 63

15. Jensen Bond 68

16. The Ledwinka Lancias 74

17. MG Landcrab Love 78

18. The Real Italian Job 83

19. Horseless Gas Carriage 88

20. When Mercedes bought NSU 93

AutoFutropolis – Car History Rebooted

21. Those Bargain Renault Porsches 98

22. When Rolls were really Jags 103

23. The Routemaster Family 107

24. Saab's very own Elk 111

25. Nissan Scimitar Makes the Cut 115

26. Sinclair's Electric Dreams Come True 119

27. Siva Moon Buggy takes off...124

28. Trab Trab Sputnik 129

29. Tucker The Swiss Carmaker 133

30. When TVR went 4×4 137

31. Vanden Plas in the USSR 142

32. Standard Go Off Road 147

33. Welcome to the Jet & Computer Age 151

34. Vauxhall Vulcan Out of this World...156

35. Conceptualism - when manufacturers thought out of the boring old saloon/hatch/estate/pick-up box... 165

36. That time I 'drove' a concept that became reality 179

Autofutropolis – Car History Rebooted

Autointroduction

Sometimes the truth hurts. Occasionally it is stranger than fiction, quite often it is too hard to handle. However, fiction is fun. It gives your imagination the opportunity to go absolutely anywhere, making stuff up, but sometimes taking a set of facts then changing the outcome to create almost limitless possible endings and unexpected twists.

This is what I have tried to do here in AutoFutropolis. It is a mouthful of a title, but the alternatives, like Autoternatives didn't scan or look right graphically. If you want the title broken down, well it's all about Autos, mostly cars, in the future. When it comes to Polis, which means 'city' in Ancient Greek, that's harder to justify, but I see these imaginary stories living out their alternative outcomes in a huge futuristic Cityverse. Or something.

When it comes to cars, as an enthusiast, what could be more amusing than fiddling with historical reality? Especially when the reality was often so grim and disappointing. I've used the bright shining turd like example of British Leyland, as the ultimate in wishful thinking and rewriting of a terrible and tragic true story that is truly deserving of a happy ending. I think I've touched on BMC and BL a bit here, it is unavoidable. The rather flawed 1800 gets two mentions only because an MG magazine asked me to draw a picture of a parts bin variant. So I had to come up with a story to fit the picture. In all the other cases I did the picture last. The story always came first, then the picture. Indeed, the stories in their original form have been seen before. They seemed to go down well when published in a classic weekly newspaper called Classic Car Buyer. Several people, about three, wanted them grouped together and expanded so I was only too happy to oblige. New, improved and added to. They have been revamped, topped and tailed with an update on what really happened. I had thought that it would have been easy enough to knock out this book in a couple of days, but it turned into a very absorbing six months as everything did need rewriting, redrawing, re-imaging and adding to. Actually there are several brand new never before released stories. The last story involving the Vauxhall SRV was certainly crucial to

AutoFutropolis – Car History Rebooted

the way this book turned out. I needed a distinctive cover for this book and didn't believe any of my drawings were good enough. I rather liked the idea of using a very real concept car that could well have changed the future. Vauxhall had that very car in the distinctive shape of the SRV. I am grateful that Vauxhall went even further by not only granting me permission to use the SRV pictures, but dug out some other rarely seen images. Also the real stories also led to GKN giving permission for the wonderful Jensen FFF brochure artwork. Exposure to the real Auto Futuristic concepts meant that I thought it was worth looking at some of the real car manufacturer and design house dreams that may or may not have turned into reality, which is the final chapter.

I think my drawing skills are fairly average and you can have fun or alarm spotting the models I may have based some of the scribbles on. My limited imagination meant I had to be inspired by a real car and just alternativise it to fit my narrative. For each story there is an early line drawing which may not be fully inked in, suggesting how I started it. Then there would be the finished drawing at the end of the story. I had intended these to be like a display advertisement in a car magazine and mostly I have done that. Some of them look really good in colour and if you have bought the book there will be a link where you can see them in their full day glow glory. If I am really organised I may also have turned some of them into T-shirt and mug designs but we will see about that.

I surprised myself at just how broad these alternative histories are. There are vans, trikes, lorries and pretty much flying cars as well as designers with different careers, cold wars and all sorts of made up nonsense.

These stories are designed to start arguments. Please feel free to make up your own endings. Or just let me know where I've made up wrong.

Let the fibs begin.

James Ruppert 2022

AutoFutropolis – Car History Rebooted

1. E-Type spiked by the AC Dart

The Daimler SP250 'Dart' was a big departure from the limousines, saloons and special bodied roadsters that had been the company's mainstay. With the SP250 Daimler were aiming directly at the sports car market. New management, specifically ex-Triumph motor designer Edward Turner, was responsible for the change. Originally called the Dart, until American manufacturer Dodge lodged a complaint, the SP250 could not have been more different from existing Daimlers. The Triumph TR3A heavily influenced the chassis and suspension. The engine was all new, a light alloy 2.5 litre V8 that owed much to prevailing motorcycle engineering principles. Stopping it were disc brakes, a rarity at the time. It was economical, powerful and competitively priced, but it was also controversial. Not everyone liked the ornate styling, which featured pronounced rear wings and headlights. Even more radical for a Daimler was the glass fibre bodywork.

Trouble was the plastic body was not initially suited to a high performance car and modifications were soon made. B specification in 1961 resulted in a stiffer chassis and bodywork. C models from 1963 had better trim. However, since Jaguar had taken over the company they really did not need any competition for the E-Type, so production was wound down. They were never going to unload the name but when AC made some enquiries back in '61 Jaguar were keen to talk. It was the ugly runt of their

Autofutropolis – Car History Rebooted

litter and sales were only trickling towards 2000 so why not flog the ugly duckling off?

Now AC were minnows in the manufacturing scheme of things and Jaguar were happy to supply engines for a while and maybe enter into some sort of licensing deal to manufacture the engine in the future. Right now though as 1963 became 1964, AC were poised to launch their very own Dart at the world.

What they had already done was finally make the car pretty. Speaking to the GRP experts Lotus helped, and it was a small matter of beefing up whatever Chapman said by at least two or three times. Most of all though they had to make it beautiful. So why they were hanging around Lotus it seemed like a good idea to chat to Lotus' accountant Peter Kirwan-Taylor who had made such a good job of the Elite. And a with the Elite, AC commissioned aerodynamicist Frank Costin to work his magic.

What AC got was a shape, which was every bit as gorgeous as the E-Type. What had once been beaten with the ugly stick was now heart stoppingly beautiful.

Available as both a convertible and a coupe' it was an immediate hit, but AC had to be clever about this. There was a huge demand, not just in the UK and Europe, but especially in the United States. AC in their Thames Ditton factory could barely cope as it was, but they knew where the real money was, and that was across the pond. So the cleverest thing that they could do was enter into a licensing agreement with none other than Studebaker.

Studebaker was already building the unique Avanti and could see the value of having another model in their range, even if it was only distantly related. At least it was prettier than the distinctive, but awkward car they were offering which clearly wasn't going to be as successful as they had hoped. So out went Raymond Loewy's controversial design and in came another less controversial four-door version of the Dart.

We are digressing and can come back to the Avanti at another time. For now the Studebaker AC alliance was making serious amounts of money and helping to get AC back on track and dominate endurance racing in Europe and America. Not only that, Studebaker had better lawyers, so the Dart name was back.

AC learnt a lot from the Dart because instead of just making the hand finished Cobras for their usual clients there

AutoFutropolis – Car History Rebooted

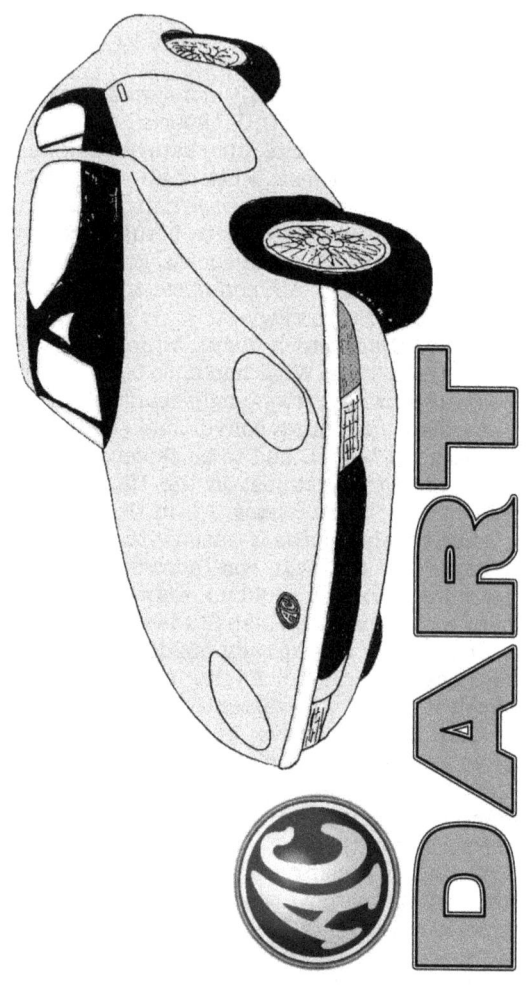

was a whole generation of new customers who appreciated the better value, equally light, but cheaper models, based on the Cobra but made out of plastic and powered by those big V8 engines. So there was a major distinction between the USA ACs and the GB ACs. The ones in the States were plastic and the ones from Thames Ditton were beaten aluminum. It was the oddest of marketing plans and it seemed to work perfectly. Buyers understood there were two different, but also very similar products and neither undermined the other.

Jaguar was incandescent that a version of the Daimler V8 was still being used under the licensing agreement and wanted to terminate it. Fortunately Studebaker had been developing their own small block V8s and with the supercharging options the top of the range engines produced over 600bhp.

AC in Thames Ditton have become every bit as respected as Porsche, concentrating on building customer race cars and bespoke road cars. The Studebaker Alliance in the USA made sexy sports cars, which combined the best of British and American, engineering and sold profitably.

To this day AC remains the oldest British owned car maker. The Dart is still at the core of its range and even the revived Jaguar F Type struggled for attention against this most iconic of international sports cars.

Autoreality: Death of the sporty Daimler

The Daimler V8 was the last all new car to be produced by the company. Jaguar Cars pounced and purchased the company and paid £3.4m in May 1960. There was problem in the States with Chrysler because of the Dart name, so SP it was. Jaguar though wasted no time at all in revising the Daimler to strengthen the chassis and cure the irritating body shake.

These revised models came out towards the end of 1960, best known as the 'B' spec. The details included beams running in addition to the main chassis rails from the inner rear wheel arch to pretty much the front wheel arch. Not only that there was extra bracing inside the cockpit. So it put on weight, but was less juddery.

Then in early 1963, the 'C' spec arrived which was just the 'B' with more standard equipment. Like a cigar lighter and heater demister. The police bought them for high

AutoFutropolis – Car History Rebooted

speed pursuit purposes and although Jaguar were just happy to have the Daimler brand and limousine market, they did consider a replacement.

It was going to be called the MKII or SP252 and a couple of prototypes still exist although the project was cancelled. It was restyled of course and looked not unlike an MGB roadster and an E-Typesque cockpit.

There is always a chance that there will be more Daimlers. It is up to Tata who also own Lanchester. Not sure that anyone really cares.

Sorry, no space to squeeze in the complicated decades old AC story, maybe in Autofutropolis 2...

2. AMC Pacer, full steam ahead...

Here is the car that saved American Motors and helped make it the world leading energy conglomerate it is today.

The Pacer was a weird little concept that originally dated back to 1971 as "Project Amigo." Essentially the future of the car, or in American, 'automobile' was very much in question because of all sorts of exciting new Federal regulations. The proposed safety and emissions standards seemed almost impossible to meet. The proposed crash standards included requirements for 50 mph front impacts and rollover accidents. Meanwhile, the upcoming emissions standards threatened to make the conventional four-stroke internal combustion engine obsolete, but we will come to that later.

What the design team decided was that in the near future even more people would live in urban areas that would become very crowded and that meant much more agile and compact cars would be the order of the day. Indeed, the Japanese were already showing the way with Datsuns, Toyotas and Mazdas, which were proving very successful as second, third, or just student cars.

For an American motor the car was small and stumpy. With the urban freeways in mind it was only 171 inches long, that's 4,356mm is Euro terms. However, it was on the wide side at 77 inches (1,963mm), giving a lot more elbow room for the driver and passengers. They also had a brilliant view out thanks to the huge expanse of glass, so they would be happier and safer. Getting in and out was easier and safer for all passengers thanks to the nearside door being noticeably longer. Then to top and tail it all, was the hatchback, a new fangled European idea for getting the mall shopping back home easier.

With all that forward thinking being applied to what would become the Pacer, the propulsion technology would be equally futuristic. The engine needed to be economical, cause the minimal amount of pollution and be reliable. Instead American Motors had prepared the car for a two-rotor Wankel rotary engine. In practice it would be smaller, lighter and smoother than a conventional piston engine, but otherwise it would deliver far worse miles to the gallon. Not only that, although the Wankel produced fewer oxides of nitrogen its hydrocarbon and carbon monoxide emissions were higher than a piston engine. Also rotor tip reliability was an issue. So AMC did the unthinkable and cancelled the deal with General Motors for the engine. The really easy option would have been to adopt existing piston engines. Instead AMC went for broke, or rather steam.

There wasn't much space under the bonnet after being prepped for the Wankel, but AMC acquired the rights to the Pritchard Steam Power engine invented by Australian engineer Edward Pritchard. The unit consisted of a condensing steam power plant that used a steam generator and a uniflow engine mounted behind it, in a two cylinder in a 90-degree V pattern. No gearbox was required it was attached directly to the driveshaft. Remarkably the engine did not need to idle, so at the traffic lights it just switched off, meaning that the exhaust emissions were zero. The fuel used for the burner was kerosene, or jet fuel. However, the burner only needed to be on for very short periods, when accelerating or firing up and rarely stayed on for longer than 10 seconds. Warm up from cold was just 30-seconds.

There was an awful lot more to the Pacer Steamer than this, but it worked and although the American public needed a lot of reassurance and persuasion the sheer novelty of the system and the lovable, cuddliness of car itself won it many fans. Especially in California where the anti-smog legislation was starting to bite. Residents of the State were happy to adopt such an environmentally friendly power plant and prove to the world that the whole steam concept really worked. The steam graphics were all part of

the fun. AMC switched all their vehicles to this hugely refined steam technology. Incorporating turbines to improve power output and a unique anti-freeze into the working fluid meant that these vehicles could be used in any region of world, not just the friendly climate of California.

Within just a few years AMC were making millions of profitable models that could be as unusual as they wanted to be, because they worked and they delivered economy and the lowest emissions. Indeed, AMC scaled up their steamer technology to power and heat homes and cities. All thanks to the podgy little Pacer.

Autoreality: Off the Pacer

American Motors always struggled and the . *The First Wide Small Car* was a weird way to promote the odd looking glass bubble of a car. It was a hit initially but could not sustain that momentum. Not least because some of the engines were underwhelming.

Anyway the prospect of a Wankel transplant was a very real one, but it didn't happen as the world slipped into fuel crisis mode. That meant AMC needed a rethink and slight re-engineer to squeeze in the straight 6 that powered all the other AMCs from Gremlin to Jeep Wagoneer. It got electronic ignition and rack & pinion steering with independent front suspension to make it thoroughly up to date, for an American car anyway.

Unfortunately the engines were tuned to be low emission and deliver maximum mpg. It had just the one struggling carburetor which also had to cope with an awful lot of extra weight not just because of the big old engine, but also the colossal amount of glass which accounted for over 30% of the bodywork. As sales dropped for the Coupe the Pacer Wagon three door estate didn't change very much, it just added more weight. Installing a 5.0 litre V8 hardly improved matters it added even more weight and led to the failure of the steering.

Apparently all the cars sold in in 1980 and there were 405 Coupes, and 1,341 of the Wagons, had been built the year before. This was the end of the Pacer. With the right smaller, lighter and more efficient engine it could have been a contender, but as we all know although the Pacer faded away, constantly being voted, World's Worst Car, it came back with a bang in that major motion picture: Wayne's

World.
    Wayne and Garth made the Pacer hip for the first time and now these are sought after rarities. That's even more incredible than this made up Steamy Story.

3. When Rolls Royce embraced the Black Knight

Invicta was founded in 1925 and by 1933 was bankrupt which where Rolls Royce stepped. In between those two dates they seemed to be having fun, even if financially it was a constant struggle.

Founders Noel Macklin and Sir Oliver Lyle wanted a quintessentially British Vintage car but with a flexible, almost lazy American feel by combining big engines, gearboxes and axles from existing manufacturers. These were well built and engineered cars that enjoyed a string of racing successes.

Unlike other 'bitza' car builders, the Invicta operation involved hand assembling limited numbers of high quality sporting cars. By using large Meadows six cylinder engines these cars could accelerate to 60 mph without changing out of first gear and the legendary S-Type had a top speed of 95mph.

It was a combination of the depression and very high prices, which put them out of business. For instance their 4.5 litre model cost almost £1000 which in 1929 was Rolls Royce money. By 1932 Invicta were in deep financial trouble and they believed that a cheaper and less powerful model would sell in large numbers. It didn't.

The model name, 12/45, referred to the RAC rating for horsepower and claimed horsepower, but that power output and the fact that the engine was a Blackburne could hardly shift this heavy car along fast enough. Even the later supercharged 12/90 struggled to reach 70mph. It was expensive too, because at £535 this was double what an equivalent Riley or SS (Jaguar) would have cost.

In 1933 it was ironically Rolls Royce money that bought the company. They realised that the Flying Lady justified very high asking prices so they dropped Invicta, but kept the Black Prince. Although Rolls Royce appealed to the super rich and the aristocracy there was also a large entrepreneur class in Britain and throughout the world who wanted something special. Although it was always possible to buy a chassis and commission whatever you wanted on top, Rolls Royce had looked at what SS was up to. The so-called 'Bond Street Bentley' was a huge success appealing to the self made characters who wanted Bentley style but did not want to pay the price. Well, Rolls Royce were certainly not going to devalue their Bentleys. They did though have the Black Prince.

Rolls Royce decided to take up racing and following in Invicta's impressive tyre tracks. However, it wasn't just Rolls Royce that would be funding the racing programme, The War Office would too. It had not gone unnoticed that the Nazi Party in German was effectively bankrolling The Auto Union and Mercedes Silver Arrows.

However, the rules for Grand Prix racing stated that the maximum weight could only be 750 kg which helped the innovative Germans and counted against the so-called big engined lorries that Bentley built. Rolls Royce were not going racing with Bentleys anymore, now it was the Black Prince with War Office backing. While the boffins worked hard on the racing cars, Rolls Royce could concentrate on the road cars. Well, they managed to get one model out that proved to be incredibly popular.

The Black Prince was built at a new factory in Coventry just down the road from rivals SS. There was nothing as vulgar as mass production, the high level of hand finishing meant that they could justify a profitable asking price that was comfortably above the SS. Those who could afford the Black Prince adored the provocative and very sexy styling and the relaxed power of the eight cylinder engines. This rakish coupe looked sensational whether it was cruising down Bond Street, or Wilshire Boulevard.

Meanwhile on the track, progress had been slower. The white coated scientists first priority had obviously been the war effort and it wasn't until 1938 that the Racing Black Prince emerged on the track. Painted gloss black to contrast totally with the Silver Arrows, the lightweight and ultra aerodynamic racer really looked the part. The win on the

AutoFutropolis – Car History Rebooted

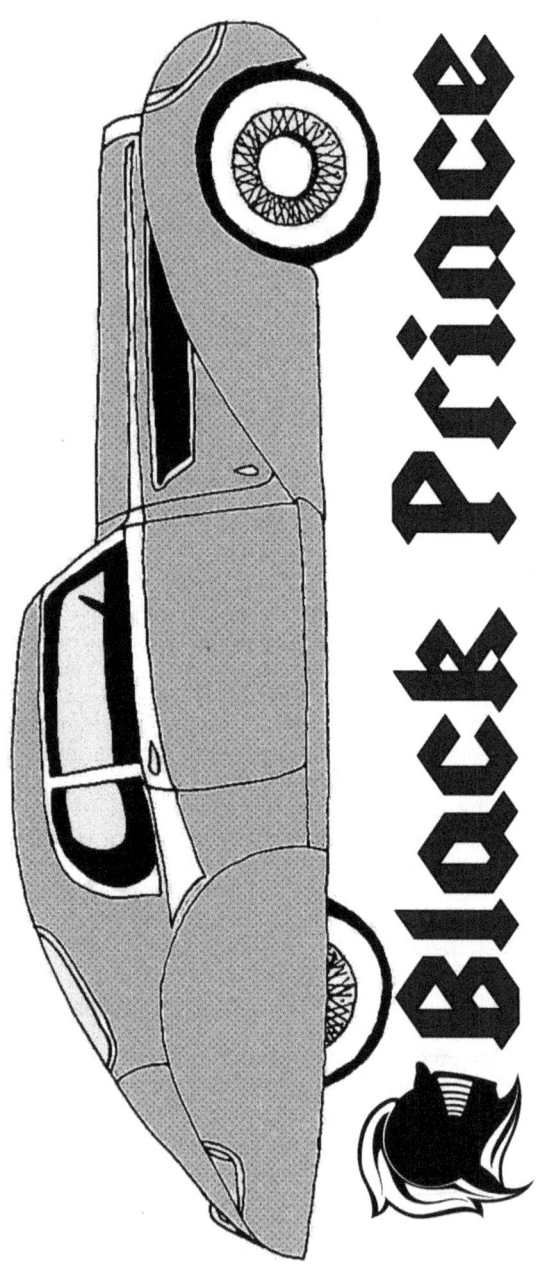

home circuit at Donington stunned everyone especially as it pushed Nuvolari's Auto Union into a distant second place.

The war though got in the way of course. The Black Prince went into hibernation along with the Racing Black Prince. Dusted off in the late '40s the Racing continued its winning ways into the 1950s. They now fought Ferrari, Mercedes and Maserati on equal terms. However, the prevailing climate of austerity meant that the road going Black Prince took a little longer to take off. When it did though the reborn Jaguar range struggled to compete. It was only a matter of time (1958) before Rolls Royce made William Lyons an offer he could not refuse and expanded the Black Prince range which now included the Invicta saloons and the new sports car Jaguar had been working on.

Autoreality: Invicta Reborn again...

Here was a car brand that was difficult to kill off. Sales certainly fell away and it shut down in September 1933, although it moved to Chelsea and where nothing happened. Meanwhile, Macklin went on to found Railton.

The first revival came in 1946 with the Invicta Black Prince, which had a Meadows engine and a complicated hydro-kinetic variable ratio gearbox and independent suspension. After just 16 cars were built, the company was taken over by Fraser Nash.

The name was acquired by enthusiast Michael Bristow in 1989, then in 1989 used the Invicta name to form a restoration and maintenance company, looking after existing Invictas. It was then decided to get back in the car building business at the British Motor Show in 2002.

The S1, remarkably was the first one-piece carbon fibre sports car, it also had a 600-horsepower Ford V8 supercar that was capable of 200 mph. Hardly any were built not least because it was furiously expensive. Between 2008 and 2012 they retailed for up to £160,000.

However, the business changed its name to the Westpoint Car Company and went bankrupt in April 2012 saving the Invicta name so that it can be reborn another day.

4. BMC Reborn: After Issigonis

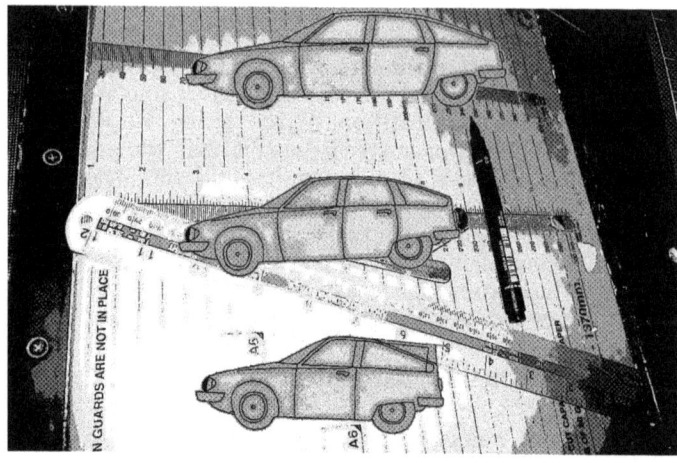

Not everyone saw the overthrow of Issigonis coming, but the Austin Morris 1800 was his undoing. Essentially this was a scaled up 1100/1300 but not quite so lovable or successful.

In 1964, the 1800 was one of the major car announcements of the year and intended to replace the myriad versions of Farina saloons. This was unmistakably an Issigonis design, and with its big MGB sports-car-related engine driving the front wheels, the rest of the body could be given over to looking after passengers. So inside, it was truly massive, and with its advanced suspension this was a successful candidate for the Car of the Year gong in 1964. It was strong, compact and heavy, but with a smooth ride.

However, whereas the 1100 and 1300 had understated bodywork courtesy of the Italians, the 1800 was also styled by Pinin Farina. However, it was seriously meddled with in Birmingham. As a result it looked dumpy and uncomfortable, and quickly gained the nickname "land crab". Issigonis's insistence on a stark interior didn't help either.

Launched first as an Austin, the model was hard to find at the dealers and quickly gained a reputation for being less than reliable. So as the gearbox and suspension played up, BMC struggled to sell 22,000 in the first year. Indeed, more buyers opted for the old Farina saloons that comfortably outsold the all-new car.

Getting rid of Issigonis was never going to be easy. As Technical Director he had a lot of power. The simple thing was to promote him out of the way to a meaningless position, Group Technical President, and then hope that out of sheer frustration he might go of his own accord. That is exactly what happened in 1966

The grand plan though was an ambitious unravelling of BMC where it was proposed to reduce everything down to core Austin Morris products and then rebrand them all as BMCs. There would be no more mergers, or badge engineering. It was hoped that this would improve dealer morale and allow the streamlining of production. George Harriman as managing director wanted to follow Ford's example by having a simpler and profitable model line up. There would be a small car, the Mini, a medium in the shape of the 1100/1300 and large which would be the 1800, later 2000. It was a radical and controversial plan and the bedrock of the changes was a revamp of all the models mentioned. Pininfarina were put in charge of styling the cars and given a completely free hand, something that Issigonis would never have allowed.

Meanwhile all the competing brands were gradually phased out to be reborn as BMCs. Pininfarina were extremely keen to change the look of what had been traditionally conservative models. They already had a full-sized wooden model of what was called the Aerodinamica and ploughed ahead with that.

Incredibly BMC waved this radical design through. Aerodynamic and innovative with an almost Citroensque flair, the soft wedge shape without a traditional grille or conventional three box shape, er took shape. BMC were going to have a brand new five door family car. Except that it was not going to stop there. The decision was made to launch a completely new range all at once. Three models were set to hit the showrooms in July 1969. Except that the engineers and a new breed of automotive management, called product planners, an idea borrowed from Ford, pointed out the sheer folly of doing that. So a phased introduction was agreed upon.

Already BMC had fallen out with the government that had wanted them to take on Jaguar (eventually bought by General Motors) and resisted all encouragement to link up with Leyland (merged with Scania).

When the BMC 1800 broke cover it caused something of a shock. Especially as it was accompanied by the announcement that generations of famous marques were to be discontinued. Letters were written to The Times, by retired Colonels and maiden aunts distressed that they could no longer buy themselves a Riley or Wolseley. There were also questions in the house. Reducing the workforce was arguably the most controversial aspect of the whole scheme. Things were certainly difficult for a while with industrial action and initial customer reluctance to go into the shiny old BMC showrooms with their groovy new logos. What helped win over the public was the BMC 1100/1300 a year later in 1970 and then in '71 the all-new BMC Mini. Suddenly the company had a brace of truly brilliant cars that had an international appeal. BMC could improve the quality and reliability because of their increasing profitability. There was a still a threat from Japan but it was the style and panache of the BMCs that won over the Great British car buying public who bought these models by the forecourt full and still continue to do so.

Autoreality: BMC what could have been...

An alternative view of the 1800, not a restyle but a new MG badge, some attitude, a tailgate and built properly can be found alphabetically further on in this book. However, this range restyle was based on fact, I just extended it from the 1800 and 1100 to the mini. But hey, the Turin-styling house also secretly built a Mini-based three-door 1000 prototype for BMC to a similar design, that has never been seen.

Sadly these remarkable Pininfarina styling concepts were never considered for production. Less than two and a half years after the Pininfarina 1800 Aerodinamica was shown, Citroen revealed its GS mid-size model at the 1970 Geneva Salon. It was almost identical to Fioravanti's two BMC prototypes. The GS was followed four years later by Citroen's range-topping CX,

Then came the Rover SD1 and Lancia Gamma Berlina which all looked a bit arrow shaped.

The thing is, this scenario is a proper 'what could have been' rather than me just making a load of nonsense up. It is doubtful that without a root and branch reworking of how BMC and later British Leyland operated built and marketed motors, a good looking range would not have helped very much. The SD1 was certainly good looking, whereas the 1800 was less so. Make your own mind.

5. Bricklin to the Future

Yes that's right the star of that moderately successful film was a Bricklin, the not very successful at all Canadian manufactured gull wing sports car. Businessman Malcolm Bricklin was the man who managed to persuade the Canadian government to finance production of the SV-1 to the tune of $23 million.

If that sounds incredibly familiar, well it is. Ex-General Motors John Z. De Lorean at the same time as the Bricklin was being built, 1974-5, formed DMC (De Lorean Motor Company) with Bank of America business loans, and gullible celebrities like Johnny Carson, (a Michael Parkinson type TV interviewer). De Lorean wasn't stupid enough to use his own money and also started an investment program, in which the car dealerships were made shareholders in the company. Best of all though he targeted desperate government organisations keen to subsidise any company that might bring hope and jobs to a deprived region. Des O'Malley the Republic of Ireland's Industry Minister decided against building cars in his back yard. However, switching to the warmer climes of Puerto Rico, De Lorean got a more favourable response and more money.

However, for a time the car company were going to skip north of the Irish border as the promise of much more money from NIDA, the Northern Ireland Development Agency, put $135m on the table. Colin Chapman though came to his country's rescue and his own of course. The early prototypes, and there were only two) were shockingly bad. Chapman didn't really know where to start when it came to how poor the De Lorean would be. Analysis revealed at just 26 mph if the De Lorean was hit from behind the engine would end up on the driver and passenger's laps. Or what was left of their laps. Those gull wing doors may have looked good, but were difficult to fit properly.

Chapman was being paid by De Lorean, well sort of. It was General Products Development Services Inc registered in Panama, who wrote the cheques to Lotus, but Chapman was looking at the much bigger figures. So instead of De Lorean operating in Northern Ireland, why couldn't Lotus? Here was an opportunity to make an established British car to earn valuable export dollars. Indeed Chapman reckoned that if the factory just made USA spec Esprits that would be the perfect way to get his cars subsidised and also heavily promoted. The Americans would love the idea of a sort of Shamrock Lotus.

So for an easy life the Government agreed, because the more they looked into De Lorean the less they liked what they saw. Unknown in Blighty he was a legendary figure in the American motor industry. From what anyone could gather his one clever idea was dropping a largish engine into a smallish car to create the Pontiac GTO. However, with an ego the size of a planet and his surgically enhanced features he was all about style rather than substance and it was hardly surprising that his vanity dictated that he should want to stick his name on the front of a car. Now he could do that in Puerto Rico.

This is the point when the De Lorean story splits into two. The factory in Dunmurry became a full time Lotus production facility aimed principally at the United States. Meanwhile, over in Puerto Rico the DMC-1 took shape. Out went the gull wing doors, the Peugeot-Renault-Volvo fuel-injected, aluminum 2.8-liter V-6 engine and the brushed stainless steel skin. Essentially what John De Lorean wanted to do was resurrect a 1964 prototype called XP-833, later known as the Pontiac Banshee. He went back to his old employers, General Motors, in search of a suitable engine. However, they were already quite far advanced with their own plastic project known internally as the P-car. This was supposed to be an economical commuter vehicle which had evolved into something a bit sportier.

General Motors quickly realised that De Lorean had no usable car, money, or anything that was really useful to them apart from government backing to build a facility

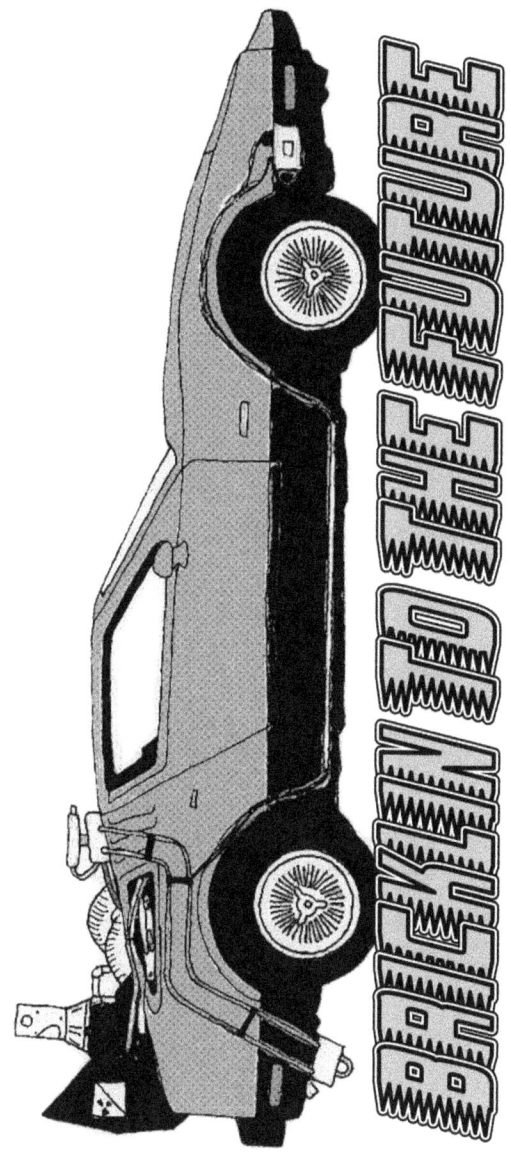

somewhere warm. For a while they considered using the De Lorean name on their own project to slightly distance them from it should everything end in tears. In the end they used some of Giorgetto Giugiaro's design which meant their P-Car became much larger. De Lorean was easily ousted and the DMC-1 soon became the Pontiac Fiero. Many saw it as a much cheaper alternative to the more exotic Northern Irish built Lotus Esprit.

That competition actually inspired Pontiac to invest heavily and really develop their grown up Fiero to the point where it became America's most popular sports car. Meanwhile the higher quality build and finish of the Northern Irish Esprits led to production of all models being transferred from Norfolk.

As for that film, (Bricklin to the Future) well it was reasonably successful, but Charlie Sheen may not have been the best choice for the lead role and Donald Sutherland as the Doc was similarly miscast. So much like the Bricklin and De Lorean, there were no sequels.

Autoreality: Lack of a Future

I'm sure I don't have to explain just how successful Back to the Future was and II and III. However, I never had the opportunity to explain to Universal Pictures that the image they can see on these pages is a bit of gag, a play on words even. Except that they managed to strike the image from a T-shirt and Mug site without giving me the right of reply.

I thought I'd explained a lot more about the Bricklin, but no that was certainly more a DeLorean story and we all know how that actually ended, in bankruptcy, court and some Bolivian marching powder. The true story of the Bricklin is actually no less interesting or complicated and it is worth looking into how this remarkably similar vehicle came about. Things could have been different for Lotus too, but they stayed in Norfolk.

Malcolm Bricklin was a clever businessman who was big in hardware and imported the first Subarus to the USA. Mostly though he is best know as the creator of the world's first safety sports car called the Bricklin SV-1 in 1974. It wasn't that well developed or built, and less than 3,000 safety sports cars saw the light of day before it all ended in tears, in 1975. Powered first by an AMC V8, then a Ford and assembled in Canada, the Bricklin pioneered some interesting concepts. There was a clever system to make the body using acrylic and vacuum forming process, which bonded color-impregnated acrylic to each fibreglass body panel. On the safety side it had impact absorbing urethane 5mph bumpers, a built-in roll cage, side bars, and a heavily protected fuel tank. The gullwing doors were also marketed as being safe as they opened out of the way of traffic. Also, because Bricklin believed that smoking was bad for you, there was no cigarette lighter or ashtray. He had a point.

6. Chrysler goes full Airflow

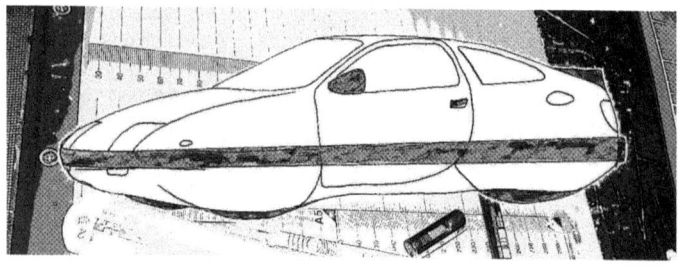

The Chrysler Airstream's radical design saw the wings fared into the bodywork and the headlights also become part of the car. The bonnet extended down to the front axle and had horizontal louvres. This monocoque rather than separate chassis built range was truly striking, indeed it proved rather too striking for the American buying public.

It was slightly better received in the UK where Chrysler had set-up an importation and assembly operation, on the banks of the River Thames in Kew, Surrey. Chrysler Motors Limited imported Chryslers, De Sotos and Plymouths and renamed them after 'local' towns. There were fixed head, drophead and saloon versions of the Richmond Airstream Six, Kingston Airstream Eight and Croydon Airflow De Soto. The Airstream name was a problem anyway because of the caravan manufacturer. Chrysler UK were brave and decided to continue the experiment when US production finished importing the tooling and drawings. They decided to press ahead with limited production for the European market. Trouble is, this was 1938 and by 1939 there was a war on and the Airflow range was mothballed.

Post war there was a rush to get back to building cars, but it would be the old models first and Chrysler dug out the Airflows. However, steel was rationed it didn't look like they could make very many. Instead Chrysler chose lightweight unrationed aluminum for the bodywork. That meant rengineering a simple tubular chassis into the equation. However, with many skilled men and women used to making aircraft, they could rivet anything together to the highest standards. Although virtually hand built, it was completed on a scale that made it cost effective and a big hit. Premium priced over an Auntie Rover, doctors, architects and lawyers lapped up the futuristic Chrysler Airflow.

Suddenly the Airflow styling looked fresh and modern in the post war era. The largish engines made them very quick combined with the weight saving aluminum and obviously aerodynamic bodies. Chrysler dropped the quaint town names and stuck with Airflow and the engine size. However, the American company could see that if they were to grow they could not go on hand building cars in the same way.

It was now the middle 1950s and Chrysler struck up a conversation with Colin Chapman who was making a name for himself with his sporty little cars and adventures in motor racing. On the one hand there did not seem to be much that Chapman could do for Chrysler. However, by applying his principles of lighter weight and even more advanced aerodynamics this would give the Airflow a new lease of life. Chapman smoothed out the bodywork and applied some tricks he had learnt from racing. Most of all though he proposed fibreglass bodywork and much smaller and more efficient sporty engines.

The timing could not have been better as the Suez fuel crisis hit. It was all very well for someone to go and buy a Bubble car, but what would middle class families drive? That would be the 1.0 litre Chrysler Airflow which could return an astounding for the time, 40 mpg, even more if they coasted and drove sympathetically. The Airflow thrived and also helped the growth of Lotus with the high performance Lotus Airflow versions.

Airflows still didn't make a lot of sense back home in America so the model was Europe only and remained a range of saloons, coupes and dropheads. Chrysler made sure that Airflows were always at the cutting edge of automotive technology and were early adopters of anti skid brakes and all wheel drive, whilst the efficiency of the core models helped them ride out subsequent fuel crises in the '70s. Their quantum leap though was when they made contact with Professor Eric Laithwaite in the mid 1970s.

He had been working with the British Government to develop a unique form of propulsion. Budget cuts saw that terminated, so he was a genius at a loose end. Essentially his linear motor was levitated by electromagnetism providing quiet, efficient magnetic suspension over a maintenance-free track. That generated the electricity to power the magnetic lift of the track from the movement of what would have been

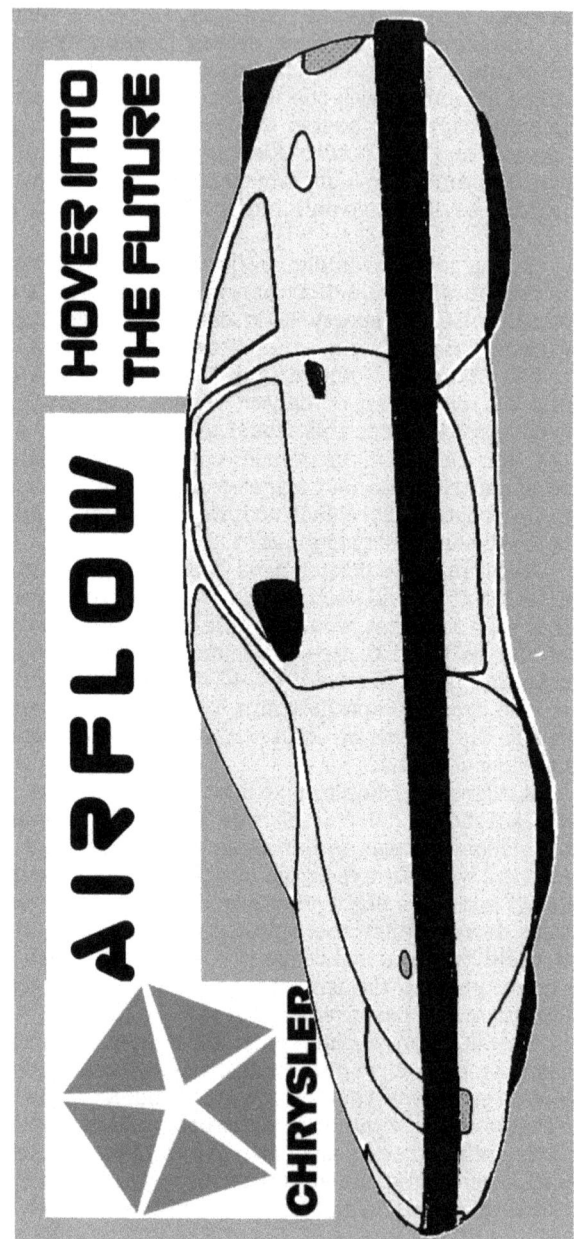

a

train. Incredibly Laithwaite then managed to develop the system to the point where the engine could get the lift from a self-generating magnet field below the vehicle. He had invented the hover car with the magnetic levitating, or Maglev system. 1980 was year zero for personal transportation.

The Chrysler Airflow did not just reinvent the wheel, but do away with it altogether. The future of motoring is now hovering over a road near you.

Autoreality: The Airflow truth...

Back in the early 1930, engineers Owen Skelton, Carl Breer, and Fred Zeder, sometime referred to as The Three Musketeers were thinking outside of the usual design parameters. At that time they were conducting wind tunnel tests with the cooperation of aviator Orville Wright to discover the most efficient shape. Apparently the conventional two-box design of cars was more aerodynamically efficient, provided it was turned backwards.

In 1934, Chrysler introduced the DeSoto and Chrysler Airflow cars. There were production problems and quality issues that hurt sales. Chrysler then Desoto sold a parallel line of more conventional cars, called Airstream which cost more. Not a success.

Professor Eric Laithwaite was quite simply a genius. He was a world authority and inventor of the linear motor. Although it could and did power the Maglev train (at Birmingham Airport which was just 600 metres long) it was expensive and there was never the infrastructure to support it.

7. The Supersonic XJ

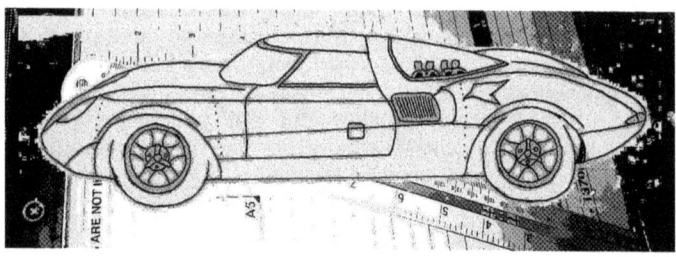

The story of Concorde is very well known. Developed and built by British and French engineers as the British Aircraft Corp and France's Aerospatiale worked together to build the supersonic sensation.

The name Concorde was chosen as, in both French and English, means agreement. British Prime Minister Harold Macmillan, decided to remove the 'e' from the end, as he was annoyed that his French counterpart, Charles de Gaulle, cancelled a meeting with him. In December 1967 as the aircraft was rolled out for public display Minister for Technology, Tony Benn, renamed it Concorde again. Claiming that the 'e' stood for Excellence, England, Europe and the so-called Entente Cordial, Benn also had another idea. It was decided to promote the supersonic aircraft by commissioning a very, very fast car or two. One built in Britain and the other in France.

Benn had encouraged the creation of BLMC in 1968 and it was a condition that the new company make a supercar to complement the supersonic plane. The French ministers made the same request towards their state owned industry who were very reluctant to co-operate with Brits. The feeling was of course, mutual.

BLMC had enough on its plate trying to bring together so many disparate companies. There was however a quick fix, the Jaguar XJ13. Built as a potential Le Mans contender, it never competed in any race. Sadly it had become obsolete as Le Mans regulations only allowed prototype cars with engines of up 3 litres. To run cars with larger engines, manufacturers had to build fifty examples as production cars. So here was a way of getting back into motorsport in a big way, but government money was going to be needed to make that happen.

The car itself was remarkable and aerodynamicist Malcolm Sayer who had also been responsible for the C-type and D-type had designed another fabulous car. The 502bhp, 5-litre V12 engine was outstanding and during early testing in 1967, it lapped the MIRA test track at over 161mph, establishing a lap record in the hands of racing driver David Hobbs.

Jaguar then had a ready built car that still needed plenty of development, but at least they had a plan. Over in France there wasn't much chance that they could compete. It would have been difficult to design a better looking car, so they didn't try. Renault obviously asked their sporting arm, Alpine to come up with a glassfibre version. They took a look and agreed the XJ13 was pretty, but not as handsome as their own A110. At least it had a proper roof. They were not even going to the bother of shoehorning in that great big Jaguar V12 when they had a Le Mans prepared example which could be renamed.

So both countries took the easy option, which meant when Concorde 001, (built in France) made its first test flight on March 2nd 1969 in France, both vehicles were there to hammer down the runway (the XJ13 in BOAC colours) as a prelude to the main event. It happened again when Concorde 002 (built in the UK) flew on April 9th 1969.

Whereas the Jaguar XJ13 Concord was still a one off, with no firm plans to take it racing, the Alpine Concorde was a mainstream model and available in designated Renault showrooms.

Unfortunately Alpine struggled to make more then ten cars a week. However, after the high profile pictures and news footage of both cars, the demand worldwide for the Alpine in general and the XJ13 in particular went through the roof. However, after those stunts in 1969 there wasn't much for the public, or world to get excited about as Concorde would not enter commercial service for another seven years. It was now up to the vehicles to keep everyone entertained.

Already referred to as the Jagpines by motoring enthusiasts, here were two very different cars that had the potential to be great racers even if the Jaguar in particular seemed a lot more dated especially in the 1970s, a period of Porsche 917 domination. Alpine had quite distinct racers that looked nothing like the road cars, but Jaguar did not have that flexibility. Farming out the race preparation

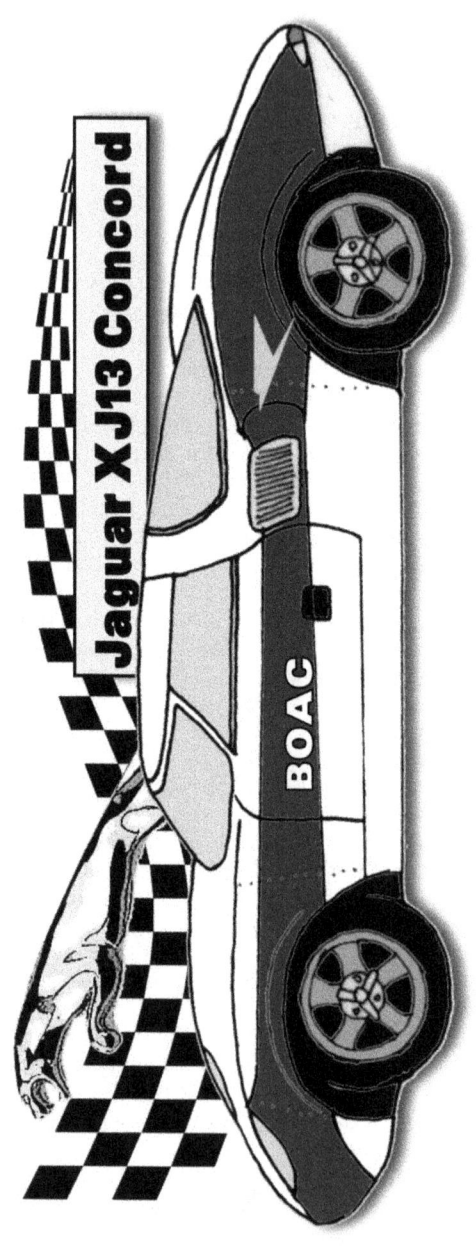

and development to Lola, while Jaguar got on the business of making enough road cars to enable them to qualify for the sports car racing.

As politics got in the way of launching the world's first supersonic passenger airliner, building enough XJ13s was a struggle as state owned British Leyland were at their lowest ebb. Never mind, they managed to get it all together long enough for a one off Le Mans victory in 1976 for the Jaguar XJ13 Concord. On January 21st 1976. British Airways flew their Concorde from Heathrow Airport to Bahrain, and Air France flew from Paris to Rio. Alpine's Concorde triumphed in 1978.

Lucky owners of Jagpines have some of the rarest and most historically significant cars ever and unlike the grounded Concorde, they can still be enjoyed.

Autoreality: Concorde the real Droop Snoots

Well, it is not as if there was a car with Concorde as the model name. Except there was. Sort of.

To commemorate the 10th anniversary of the first commercial passenger flight of the Concorde in January 1986, Air France wanted flight crews to use special Citroën CXs. They ordered twelve CX 25 GTi Turbos in Blanc Nacré (pearl white) paint with the interior materials as used inside Concorde. The unique paint colour caused Citroen issues and Air France cancelled the order.

Six examples were built with Concorde tail fin colours on the tailgate as a tiny logo. Apparently three were used by Citroën executives and destroyed, either by the execs or once they had finished. The others went into the dealer network and just a couple survive.

That's one more than the one and only Jaguar XJ13. Then that one XJ13 came out of retirement from under a dust sheet in 1971 returning to the MIRA test track as part of a film to announce the new E-type V12. Jaguar test driver Norman Dewis got a puncture on the banking resulting in a rather serious crash. Dewis was quick thinking enough to switch off the ignition and insert himself into an effective safety cell below the dashboard. The car was rebuilt and demonstrated at the British Grand Prix at Silverstone in 1973.

It is excellent news that the Alpine marquecame back to universal acclaim and it is not too late for Renault to introduce a proper Concorde special edition. I'm sure they will get the colour right first time.

As for the XJ13 what a lovely looking supercar it was...well still is.

8. If Colin had Built Bungalows...

It is 1948 and Colin Chapman, as he then was, is finding that the savage winter of 1947 had really taken its toll on the little engine block of his 1930 Austin 7. Although he had plans to modify and use in local trials events by stressing each panel and reducing the amount of weight to a minimum, he had a better idea. As well as cracking eggs in the radiator to prolong the block's life he was going to concentrate on transferring what he had learnt mucking about with cars, to house building.

Chapman may have gained his structural engineering degree a little late, but it was his employment with the British Aluminum Company (BAC) that convinced him that metal was the future. Indeed, in the rationed post war era, aluminum was a metal not subject to any restrictions. He felt that aluminum buildings would be easy to construct yet incredibly strong. Not only that they were far more stylish and durable than the useful, but grim prefabs. So Chapman left BAC and patented the construction methods. So called 'Chapman Streets' soon sprang up around the Britain and the world. This gave Chapman the financial freedom and independence to take on a variety of prestigious international civil engineering projects.

In the world of motorsport it was Cooper Cars who were setting the agenda and their remarkable cars and even more remarkable driver Jim Clark. Having changed the face

of motorsport with Jack Brabham who won the world title in 1959 and 1960 with Cooper, then went on to start his own racing car company in 1962. Cooper Cars signed up the brilliant Jim Clark.

Despite John Cooper's great friend Issigonis asking him to evaluate and even develop his Mini, it was Formula 1 that demanded his full attention. Ferrari fought back for a couple of years before Cooper and their brilliant designer Owen Maddock took the initiative. There were some technical dead ends, most notably the development of a twin engined layout that increased grip, but added far too much weight. However, it was the adoption of the Ford Cosworth engine and Maddock's enthusiasm for hovercraft design and engineering that led to a domination of the Formula.

Downforce was the key and little understood at the time, unless like Maddock you knew exactly how hovercrafts work. As much as he wanted the Cooper T2000 to float frictionless down the straights on a cushion of air and then be steered precisely around corners by tiny almost castor like wheels, that didn't happen. No, a complex series of ducts and rotors created a unique way of keeping on the track. Allied to Jim Clark's superlative driving skill they were unstoppable. With that domination (World Champions in '63, '65, '68, '69, 70) came success and sponsorship as the world's biggest brands competed to place their logos on the wide flat flanks of the Cooper. The Corgi Kellog's Cornflake Cooper was on every car mad boy's Christmas must have wish list in 1968.

However, It was off the track that Cooper really started to shine with their own road cars. First of all they took the simple ingredients of their original Jap motorbike engined Formula three cars offering them to the public as self assembly kits. These Cooper T700s became incredibly popular especially amongst the amateur racing community. They were street legal too and offered a real racing car for the road experience which made the MGs and Triumphs of the period seem so slow and terribly old fashioned. America really could not get enough of them which funded Cooper's move upmarket.

Lightweight rear engined road cars pitched Cooper directly against Ferrari and their Dino. The Cooper T970 though was cheaper, lighter, faster and they were the world champions. However they used a Ford 1600 crossflow engine that was thoroughly reworked by Broadspeed to produce a version that produced an astounding 120bhp. Oh yes and they had to go to Italy to make it look suitably sexy and Giorgetto Giugiaro was only too happy to oblige. His recently formed Ital Design company came up with a superbly evocative style that made it as desirable as the E-Type.

Cooper kept a close eye on US vehicle regulations and most importantly established a respected dealer network to sell their cars which were a variation on a theme of the T970 and that included a four-door version with the engine from the Capri RS3100. Except that the V6 engine had Cooper cam covers and for the buyers that meant a huge amount.

As Cooper became a premium car maker the T700 had to go. The rights to make and market the kit and fully built back to basics racing cars went to a dealership called Caversham Garages. These days everyone who wants a proper sports car will get themselves a Caversham Cooper. To this day they still sell variations on the T700 theme to worldwide acclaim.

Back to racing, Cooper's number one driver Jim Clark retired in the late 1960s and like Brabham formed his own racing team that went onto great success in the '70s and '80s and Clark fought against other notable ex Formula One driver teams McLaren and Brabham. Of course it was the battles between Cooper and Ferrari that still grabbed the imagination and attention of the public as they swapped titles.

Meanwhile Colin Chapman, without many day to day stresses and with a preventative heart bypass operation in the late 1980s has enjoyed a good standard of health that has allowed him to continue working almost constantly. He has produced some truly astounding architectural wonders including the Lotus Bridge across the Thames and the amazing Wembley Europa Stadium.

Sir Colin Chapman is now 85 years old (at the time of original publication) and is still designing all sorts of exciting structures. He has a retrospective of his most prestigious designs and commissions organised by the Royal Institute of British Architects at the South Bank Centre.

Autoreality: Maybe Colin Flew South?

I rather liked the idea that Cooper went on to dominate '60s Formula 1 that Jim Clark survived to drive another day, but you've read all that. The real history of Lotus is so well known, it does not need repeating.

One interesting avenue of conjecture has been, did Colin Chapman actually die in 1982? It seems very far fetched and might be as fanciful as the story I have just concocted, but there are some strange circumstances surrounding his departure from planet earth.

The official cause of death was a heart attack, despite Chapman having just passed a check-up at Lloyd's in London for the renewal of his life insurance policy and pilot's licence.

Apparently, there was no evidence of Chapman's return from Paris to Norwich Airport in his private plane the night before he died. His burial was pretty nifty, as both Emerson Fittipaldi and Mario Andretti wanted to attend the funeral, but he had already been interred. And finally, the doctor who signed Chapman's death certificate also disappeared/died soon after. Why though would Chapman want to fake his own death?

Well, some of the money given by the British government to John DeLorean to build that ethical sports car seems to have gone missing. In January 1982, the British government discovered that 23 million pounds, almost half the funds received in 1974, had been transferred to a Panamanian account under the name of General Product Development Services. This was the company which backed Lotus.

This intrigued the FBI and the British Police conducted one interview with Chapman before he died. When the case came to court in Northern Ireland the judges indicated that the Lotus boss would have been subject to a 10 year sentence. Indeed, his right hand man Fred Bushell did go to prison without implicating his old boss.

The FBI went in search of Chapman in Brazil and much was made of his wife Hazel spending a month in Brazil after the 1983 Grand Prix, especially as she had not flown or travelled anywhere for a decade.

There is speculation that Chapman later moved to Argentina. It is a theory and one that the BBC followed up in a documentary. This is of course pure speculation, but interesting nonetheless.

9. That Time De Tomaso won Le Mans

Ford took rejection very badly. At the beginning of 1963 Henry Ford II and Lee Iacocca approached Ferrari with a view to buying the marque. What better way to get into GT racing and possibly road cars? The idea was to form two companies out of a merger. Ford-Ferrari would build and sell the kind of luxurious sports and GT cars, like Ferrari's road cars with Ford in the marketing driving seat. When it came to Ferrari-Ford, Ferrari would be very much holding the racing steering wheel of the racing team. Ford was looking ahead and also wanted to pick up the rest of Ferrari in the event that the team leader, Enzo, passed away.

Ford came very close, but the deal fell through at the last minute. Apparently it was a combination of Ford's determination to stand by Carroll Shelby's performance brand and their coolness towards Formula One meant that Enzo said no.

Instead, Henry Ford II and Lee Iacocca decided to create their own racing team and build a sports racing car that would win the legendary Le Mans 24 hour endurance race and rub Enzo's nose in it. They looked around world and found that really they did not have to stray very far from Ford's British operation in Dagenham. In fact they went to the other side of London to sunny Slough. Obviously the UK was chosen because it was regarded as a centre of excellence for the motor sport industry. Although styled at Ford headquarters in Dearborn the actual glassfibre body was moulded in England and the cars assembled at Ford's Advanced Vehicle factory, which was in Slough. The heart of the car was a Lola based V8 engined prototype designed by Eric Broadley. John Wyler from Aston Martin was appointed to co-ordinate the whole construction and racing programme.

Then Iacocca stood back. If Ford were going to get into the GT racing business they needed a more exotic name. Sadly they were never going to sell big-ticket GT cars with the blue oval on it. First of all they spoke to Ferruccio Lamborghini. He had issues with Ferrari too. Ford found him just as frustrating to deal with as Ferrari. Lamborghini was not interested in motorsport and didn't need the money that was being offered. So after being frustrated by several months of fruitless negotiation they went back to Plan B. Even though they didn't exactly have a Plan B.

Instead they called up Carroll Shelby who had been working on a Ford V8 powered car with Alejandro de Tomaso. It was going to be a mid-engined sports car, but the project did not progress as planned. Shelby told Ford that the De Tomaso sports car wasn't very good, however the man himself was ambitious to achieve racing success.

Iacocca and Ford II found that de Tomaso was a man they could do business with. When the Argentinean saw the Ford project in the metal he knew that it he would have to lend his name to it as he saw the much bigger picture. Although Ford were keen to buy the de Tomaso name, he wasn't about to sell it and just wanted a marketing deal to sell his cars with Ford power and Ford backing. The arrangement would suit everyone.

So Ford went racing with the De Tomaso name and everyone was happy, except Ferrari. Ford painted their cars bright yellow, not just to stand out, but more importantly to outshine Ferrari. This they did on the track by winning all the big endurance races from Sebring to Nurburgring and ultimately Le Mans.

What both Ford and de Tomaso wanted was to transfer the incredible success on the track to the showrooms. The only way to properly productionise a racing car and make it pay, was to stamp it out in Detroit. So glass fibre panels were out and in came modified steel ones and stock Ford V8s, although they could be ordered in various states of tune. As was usual with Ford there were lots of profitable options in the showroom. No one cared that what was nominally an Italian supercar was being made in America. Oh yes and in celebration of its success it had a very simple name, 24.

De Tomaso always has been the working class sports car and since the '60s the whole range has sold

strongly around the world. Also, whenever Ford felt they needed a publicity boost they simply reinvented the 24 for a new racing generation, and routinely win Le Mans.

Autoreality: Hollywood Go Racing

The press release issued on May 22, 1963 made the position clear, "Ford Motor Company and Ferrari wish to indicate, with reference to recent reports of their negotiations toward a possible collaboration that such negotiations have been suspended by mutual agreement."

There is now a film all about the Ford and Ferrari feud, which is a very good place to start, except that it messes with the truth. Depending on where you live it is either has the title: Ford vs Ferrari, or Le Mans '66. As always you would be far better off reading a proper book. A J Baime's Go Like Hell, Ford, Ferrari and their battle for speed and Glory at Le Mans, is probably one of the best.

So where did the film go wrong, in case you plan on watching it, or wonder where you were misled. WARNING: There might be spoilers.

Well, the film shows Ford losing in its first attempt at Le Mans before returning for the 1966 victory. Actually they tried in 1964 and 1965. They missed out on a whole year. Hollywood could have mentioned that in a couple of frames which would have taken seconds.

Throughout the film Ken Miles and Carroll Shelby have a fist fight, but there is no evidence that this ever happened. They were grown ups. Hollywood probably reckoned that it showed workplace tension or something.

The bit where Carrol Shelby scares the bejesus out of Henry Ford II in a GT40 which turns the big boss into a crying, laughing wreck, never happened. It was supposed to soften the big man up to allow Ken Miles to race in Le Mans '66. In fact Ken had raced in '65 and Ford had no objection to him being behind the steering wheel. Clearly, Hollywood being overdramatic when they really didn't need to.

Also, Enzo Ferrari didn't attend Le Mans in 1966. The scenes with him being there are like most scenes in films, made up.

The film suggests that that Shelby was the first American to have won Le Mans, which he did in 1959 in an Aston Martin. As did fellow Americans Phil Hill and Luigi Chinett in 1958 and 1949 who didn't get a mention.

Inconveniently for Hollywood they drove Ferraris.

There are lots more detail mistakes about gear changes and the climax of the race not being as portrayed, but I won't spoil too much for you. Essentially, don't trust Hollywood about anything.

However Ford did return to Le Mans with a brand new GT40....

The No. 68 Ford GT of Sébastien Bourdais (FRA), Joey Hand (US) and Dirk Müller (GER) crossed the finish line at Le Mans at three o'clock, as the overall GT winner of the 2016 Le Mans 24 Hours. The No. 69 Ford GT of Ryan Briscoe (AUS), Scott Dixon (NZ) and Richard Westbrook (GB) joined the winners on the podium after scoring third place. The Nos. 66 and 67 Ford GTs finished in fourth and ninth places, respectively.

10. When Edsel became Elvis

As we all remember, one of the great automotive disasters losing Ford some $300 million, was the Edsel misadventure.

The Edsel was born out of a need for Ford to have a mid market car that owners of more basic models could aspire to. Creating a new brand name in 1957 after Henry Ford II's father Edsel, it effectively plugged the gap between the Lincoln and Mercury ranges. In theory the good value Edsel Rangers and Pacers were slightly more expensive than Fords whilst the Edsel Corsair and Citation was more costly than a Mercury. The models looked identical although the more expensive versions had larger V8 engines. Despite lots of hype, sales were slow and dealers who over ordered went bankrupt.

Something had to be done. Now these were good cars, but Ford analysts realised that it was launched at the wrong time when buyers had started to 'downsize'. Also the Edsel had a 'horse collar' grille that some found rather challenging as it resembled something that can't be mentioned in a family classic car newspaper.

Initially all that happened is that the expensive models were dropped in 1959 and the Villager station wagon was introduced, but no one is exactly sure at which point Colonel Tom Parker got involved. As we all know, he wasn't a real Colonel, and nether was his real name Parker. However Andreas Cornelis van Kuijk was undoubtedly Elvis Presley's manager. Aware of Ford's problems he had a very novel solution. Why not rename the Edsel, the Elvis?

This was not as mad a proposal as it sounds.

Certainly the King of Rock 'n' Roll had been incredibly controversial because of his overtly sexual lyrics and performances for the time. He was also controversial not least because his music also straddled racial lines too. Hardly the sort of brand ambassador Ford needed. Except that by 1958 Elvis was in the army.

After basic and advanced training Presley's overseas service took place in Germany from October 1, 1958, until March 2, 1960, as a member of the 1st Medium Tank Battalion, 32d Armor. For the first five days of that period he belonged to Company D of the battalion, and thereafter to the battalion's Headquarters Company at Friedberg. Not surprisingly middle America fell in love with one of their own. He not only appealed to the teenagers and young adults, he was now adored by their parents too.

Colonel Parker reckoned that relaunching the failed Ford at about the time that Elvis came out of the army would be perfect. This was especially so as a redesign had already been scheduled for the 1960 model year and the line-up reduced to just two models: the Ranger and the Villager, which was swiftly renamed the Cadet. These had 145bhp six cylinder, or 300bhp V8 engines and proved to be the solid foundations on which to rebuild a marque.

No one could have predicted how successful the Elvis range would become. Ford could not make enough of them initially and the Elvis name helped the company expand into a lot of new territories.

The details of the arrangement between Ford and Colonel Tom were never fully revealed. However, many speculated that it was a straight royalty deal with a percentage of all the sales with stock options and performance related bonuses. Elvis was also the honorary President of the new company, which usually involved a round of promotional activities. Except that the 'King' took a surprisingly active role in the running of the company. When it came to the design and marketing he had very strong views insisting that the cars be sporty and performance focused. And no they didn't all have Rhinestone decoration as standard.

So how did the Elvis range develop over the years? As was originally intended with the Edsel, it was an aspirational brand, the icing on the Ford cake but with a welcome twist of sportiness. The designs were unique with a dash of rock 'n' roll flash. The famous Elvis 'TCB' (taking

care of business) was a prominent chrome badge on every model. In fact, the unique Elvis take on the Pony car phenomenon was one of the most memorable of all. Significantly when the Ford Mustang got fatter and less competitive the Elvis Camarillo (named after the Camarillo White Horse) remained true to its roots throughout the '70s and '80s.

A range of focused sporty saloons, estates and coupes remained and were always the profitable core and kept the President busy. Yes Elvis Presley was inspired by the success of the company to spend less time singing and more time promoting the car brand that had his name on it. Of course he still sang from time to time, but he rationed his appearances left the rock 'n' roll lifestyle behind and concentrated on business. His hit TV show 'The King's Apprentice' inspired a generation of entrepreneurs.

At the recent North American International Auto Show in Detroit the slick haired 75 year old was as charming as ever and by far the coolest car company boss of all time as his own lightweight Camarillo version of the new Mustang wowed the crowds. As did his impromptu version of "A little less conversation..."

Autoreality: Edsel, a Camel of Car

Designed by a committee and countless numbers of buyer surveys Edsel was effectively cancelled by an economic recession in 1959. Many industry experts reckon that if launched in 1955 it would have prospered and survived and its weird looks would not have hindered sales. Most big Detroit motors were unconventional with huge wings, chrome grilles and complicated detailing. Buyers loved them. It was just that consumers would consider smaller models and the competition for large family motors was intense.

Actually sales of 63,110 Edsels wasn't half bad for a new brand in a recession year. But Ford had hoped for sales of at least 100,000. The line up was confusing though with two basic chassis having four separate series--Ranger, Pacer, Corsair and Citation which were spread over 18 different models. Indeed, there were two and four door hardtops, two and four-door saloons, convertibles and six or nine-passenger station wagons with two or four doors. Ford hurried to make the 1959 Edsel simpler basing it on their existing chassis and bodywork. Pacer and Citation models were dropped, and only one wheelbase was available. and base prices were kept low. Even a six-cylinder engine was offered as an economy model. Despite this only 44,891 Edsels were built. Then in 1960 Only a mere 2,846 Edsels saw the inside of a showroom before production ended. Ford lost $350 million.

Interviewed years later J.C. Doyle, an Edsel marketing manager said of the great American car buying public, "What they'd been buying for several years encouraged the industry to build exactly this kind of car," he says. "We gave it to them, and they wouldn't take it. Well, they shouldn't have acted like that ... And now the public wants these little Beetles. I don't get it!"

In 1995 Ford imported the European, Belgian built Mondeo and called it the Contour to replace the old Tempo model in America. It was still too small and relatively expensive, despite being good to drive so the Mondeo/Contour was discontinued in 2000. Clearly marketing cars is complicated.

As for Elvis, well he apparently shot his Pantera. Elvis purchased a yellow 1971 De Tomaso Pantera in 1974 for $2,400 as a gift for then girlfriend Linda Thompson. This is the car Elvis opened fire on several times when it broke down, or just didn't perform as expected.

Mostly though Elvis loved cars and Cadillacs in particular and gave dozens away over the years (some estimate it was as many as 200) to friends, fans and sometimes a bank clerk called Mennie L Person who he took to a showroom and said pick a Caddy.

THE EDSEL RANGER FOUR-DOOR HARDTOP

11. Gamage Go Electric

It might be hard for modern shoppers to comprehend, but once upon a time the Interweb was actually on the high street. Not along the whole street, that would be silly, but in one shop and that shop was called a department store. One of the most famous stores of this type was Gamage in London.

The business was started in 1878 by Arthur Walter Gamage. It was established in an unfashionable part of the 'eastern' West End in Holborn. He resolved to sell everything cheaper than anywhere else. So what had been a small watch repair shop became the People's Popular Emporium, Gamage's words, selling haberdashery, furniture, sporting goods, gardening supplies and utensils, camping equipment, magic tricks, and clothing.

Not only did Gamage become a huge shop, there was also a sizeable mail order business, which really was like the Internet. Instead of screen there was a large range of catalogues that customers all over the country and Empire could order from. Indeed, one of the largest sections of the 900 page doorstop tome was devoted to bicycles. Even more significantly Gamage were ahead of so many other retailers by recognising the increasing significance of motoring.

Gamage sold accessories, from clothing to lights and all sorts of motoring paraphernalia. From a Gamage branded bicycle, then motorcycle and it was inevitable that there would be a Gamage motor carriage. The actual impact of the 1903 model, which had either 7 hp Aster, or 6 hp De Dion engine was not that great. All Gamage were doing was rebranding French cars. Then in 1915 they supplied a light car with a Chapuis-Dornier engine and this model pointed a way to the future

Gamage were the first to recognise the importance of women in the car buying process and keen to make motors that were 'female friendly', that meant easy to drive and look after. The light car was a move towards that ideal. It was small, economical and the controls were on a par with a four wheeled bicycle, which is effectively what it was, but with a rather large four-cylinder engine. What was progressive and made it easier and less bothersome for the gentlewoman, was starting the engine via a cockpit mounted cable linkage.

The First World War halted Gamage's automotive ambitions, but it resumed in the 1920s when they imported the German Slaby-Beringer electric car. Gamage now had a plan. First of all they were a friendlier alternative to a traditional garage which had its origins in the blokey blacksmiths. Gamage's retail experience and determination to put the customer first gave them an advantage, especially when it came to women and those richer consumers used to a higher level of service. Something that they were willing to pay for. Gamage created a franchised network of garages around central London and the suburbs.

The Gamage name guaranteed quality and a level of service that meant cups of tea in proper china whilst the motor carriage was attended to. A collection and delivery service and comfy button down leather sofas in the waiting area. More to the point Gamage decided it was time to make a vehicle especially for London and their mainly female customers. To that end they embraced the concept of the electric vehicle.

As the world retreated from Steam and Electricity and put heir faith in the internal combustion engine, the Gamage board believed that a simple, clean and efficient electric car was the answer. These were easy to drive, with just a forward and reverse gear. Servicing was minimal but reliably profitable with annual visits and all the owner had to do was remember to plug it in every night. The 30 to 50 mile range was more than enough making it perfect for the city and the suburbs. What they also realised is that the design did not have to be conventional, with a radiator and bonnet. The batteries could be part of the floor and the

GAMAGES — THE MOTORIST'S MECCA

Ladies, the latest 1935 Electric Gamage Motorcar is here and designed by women with the modern woman in mind. Contact the Motoring Department for more details.

motors attached directly to the wheels. So they went for comfortable and upright bodywork, and an unusually panoramic high seating position. Gamage used senior female store managers in the fashion departments to design the cars. They were advertised as being styled for the modern woman, by modern women.

The fact customers could order via catalogue mean that the Gamage became a worldwide phenomenon in cities of the world. The smartest people in Paris, New York and Berlin would order their designer Gamage by mail order. Adding designer names was also great promotional tool. Even though Gamage the store shut in 1972, the franchised garages that were nationwide and electric vehicle manufacture continued.

Gamage is still considered as the premium electric vehicle which can be ordered online. Never mind its popularity in Tokyo, Milan and Barcelona, it is now Silicon Valley's most popular small electric car.

Autoreality: Electric Deliveries

Gamage genuinely sold electric vehicles as per the story, but electric delivery vehicles were also very commonplace.

Harrods' had a fleet of electric delivery vehicles that were once a familiar sight on the streets of London. The famous department store used American-built Walker electric vans in 1919. Incredibly in the 1930s Harrods renewed their fleet, but decided to design and build them in their own workshops. The one ton vans were powered by under-floor mounted batteries giving a range of sixty miles per charge. A total of sixty vans were built up to 1939. This van remained in service until 1970.

Electric delivery vehicles, otherwise known as milk floats were a very common sight in the urban towns and city areas of Britain, where short distances meant their lack of battery range is less of a problem. EVs were once an integral part of sustainable British life. People went to work on things called trams and trolleybuses and their early morning pint of milk arrived via the largest fleet of EVs in the world, better known as milk floats. They were quiet, made a low drone and a reassuring clinky noise as the bottles tapped together. Yes, they were glass bottles, because the old ones were collected by the float, taken back to the depot, cleaned and reused. Meanwhile the floats were plugged in a charged overnight on cheap rate electricity. This is decades ago, has there really been any progress?

12. Gilbern Made in Wales, still...

Located at Llantwit Fardre with a dragon on the badge, there was never any doubt that this was a Welsh company. Gilbern was the amalgamation of the founder's Christian names, GILes Smith and BERNard Friese. Smith was a Welsh car enthusiast and glassfibre specialist and Friese a German engineer.

Obviously they had glassfibre bodies and the first model in 1959 called the GT was a stylish two door, four seater coupe'. It used a variety of mechanical parts from contemporary models. The Austin A35 was one of the cars to donate its engine as well as front and rear suspension. An optional supercharger boosted the performance. Customers could have either a fully built, or DIY kit version.

The designs were neat, the engineering principles sound and the build quality excellent. They were a tiny concern and in 1968 a Welsh company called Ace Holdings, the UK's largest slot machine maker acquired Gilbern. They in turn were taken over a year later by Mecca who not only ran Bingo halls, but also the Miss World competition. In reality Gilbern had become just a small part of a large conglomerate that had to turn in a profit and that became increasingly difficult, which is where British Leyland came in.

Government money was always available to create jobs in deprived areas (see Hillman Imp and Linwood) and BL were keen on acquiring the name rather than the glassfibre technology. They reckoned that creating an assembly operation and attaching a local name to it would help brand loyalty and boost sales in Wales with Gilbern badged Allegros. It sort of worked because as the 1970s wore on, all of BL was struggling.

George Turnbull may have been responsible for getting the Morris Marina and then the Austin Allegro into production, but became very disillusioned with the whole organisation. He believed that breaking the company up and letting each marque get on with it without interference was the answer. He never got his way and resigned as the managing director of Austin Morris. What Turnbull did next was an astounding, brave and prescient: he went to South Korea.

There he helped Hyundai establish a car plant and get it running in two years, from scratch. The Hyundai Pony used second-hand technology from Mitsubishi becoming very successful and the first Korean car to be imported to Britain. First hand he saw what could be achieved by a motivated workforce, a private company and a certain amount of carefully directed state funding. Staying abroad, Turnbull's next stop was Tehran. At the Iran National Motor Company they assembled the Hillman Minx/Hunter which was reworked and rebadged as the Paykan. It became a best seller, but Turnbull left when the Ayatollah went back home.

Back in Britain, Turnbull had some job opportunities. Chrysler had an offer on the table, but he was looking towards Wales with an idea to take Gilbern out of BL control. Paying a nominal pound he took control of the operation and then set about implementing a programme of investment and industrial revival, which mirrored what he had achieved in South Korea. He negotiated with Mitsubishi, who may have had a small presence in the UK, but he convinced them that initially allowing assembly and then small scale production was a sound business move.

What Turnbull did was very clever. Although the Mitsubishi models were previous generation, they would be updated with added British touches such as different light clusters, Rostyle wheels and trim upgrades. Plus of course that distinctive dragon badge. Best of all it meant that the Invader model could come back. Underneath it may have been a Lancer Celeste but buyers loved the fact that unlike the BL models, they didn't fall apart and started first time.

By the later 1980s, full production took place at the expanded Gilbern plant and as well as being big in Wales, sales started to rival Rover and exports to Europe were on

the increase. Fully independent and having paid back government loans. Welshibitsis, as a one sarcastic journalist called them, continued to sell strongly.

Before he retired though Turnbull thought it was vital that the company begin to develop its own models. It wasn't a surprise to anyone that when MG Rover faltered in 2005 that Gilbern picked up the remnants of their former owner. Significantly they restarted production in Longbridge of the 75 and set about replacing the 25 and 45 with rather more up to date Gilberns. From then on the British car industry was safe in Welsh hands.

Autoreality: Gilbern and George the Great

A lot of wishful, even Welshful thinking there. The problem for all tiny car companies is money and the lack of it. It is an expensive business to build cars, even if at one point in 1968 when it was taken over by ACE, a Welsh firm best known for being a leading manufacturer of slot machines, surely had no shortage of small change, perhaps when they needed bigger bucks.

The cars were never cheap, in 1971 an Invader kit cost £1,767 while in drive-it-home form the Welsh sports car would cost £2,236. The economy wasn't in great shape, then putting VAT on kit cars priced them off the road. ACE itself was taken over by the huge Mecca company, an organisation more interested in dance halls, cinemas and other kinds of entertainment than in making cars. After changing hands a few times Gilbren was bankrupt and out of business in 1973.

Sir George Turnbull is a hero of the car industry and often overlooked. In 1973 Turnbull had been in charge of Austin Morris since the BMC years and had moved them into profit and in fact generated half of British Leyland's profit at the time. Unfortunately he was denied the top job. It would not have been easy, but Leyland might have had a chance. Instead he went on to create Hyundai from the ground up, to set up the Iranian motor industry before politics got in the way. Turning down Leyland to run Talbot was an incredibly tough gig.

Becoming Chairman and Chief Executive of the Inchcape Group in the 1980s which owned many dealers he was very successful and stayed there until retirement in 1991. He can be credited with applying pressure poltically and as an industry expert to the building of the Toyota factory in Burnaston.

Not surprisingly, I thought it was worth imagining what he could do with a plastic sportscar maker in Wales.

13. When Gordon Keeble saved Vauxhall from Europe

The Gordon Keeble story was simple enough. John Gordon, who ran Peerless Cars and engineer Jim Keeble simply wanted (at the suggestion of an American air force pilot) to fit a V8 from a Corvette into a Peerless to see what would happened. Keeble wanted to start from scratch, which led to the Gordon GT and then the Gordon-Keeble.

Of course there is rather more to it than that. The trouble was that although the basic idea, big V8 in a light a car was good, the technology required to keep it on the road was not so easy, especially when it came to Great British suppliers. We will come to that later.

Everything else about the Gordon Keeble was brilliant. Firstly it was handsome. Well it would be, this four-seater coupe had been designed by Giogetto Giurgiaro, at the time chief stylist at Bertone. Secondly the turtle badge, how wonderful is that? Implying slowness, yet in the right environment, (under the sea, or on the motorway) that Corvette engine helped the car get to 140mph. Indeed it could do 70mph in first gear, which after December 1965 would be the experimental national speed limit. Anyway 1965 was a bad year, not only was the national speed limit being trialed (introduced in 1967), there were striking suppliers and the fact that they were charging a paltry £3,000 for a sports car that was better than an E-Type.

After 80 cars had been built the company got into serious difficulties. Which is when Vauxhall arrived on the scene. As a General Motors subsidiary they could get access to all the proper parts to make a Gordon Keeble work properly. Plus Vauxhall senior management rather liked the idea that they had an instant premium brand that would mean they could take on Jaguar and offer a very profitable alternative.

Keeping the founders on as consultants, Gordon Keeble production was moved to what was described as the 'special shed' in Luton. They stuck with the fiberglass shell for a while and found that it was good way of training up apprentices in the mucky body moulding and finishing area. Soon they were able to make twenty-five cars a week. The most important factor was getting just enough cars into circulation to maintain interest and stimulate demand. Pretty soon it had been dubbed the Gordon Bristol. A much more affordable and many argued a more able and modern alternative to the slightly fusty gentleman's coupe.

Vauxhall knew that limited glassfibre production was something which was best left to Lotus and all the kit car manufacturers, except that the Corvette connection made them think again and copy the process used on the third generation Corvette. From 1968 all the body parts were manufactured with a press mould process, where fibreglass material and resin were shaped in a die tool that produced smoother parts more quickly. Here was a better way to make the British GT.

Then in 1973 the composition changed from fiberglass to sheet-moulded composite, which was composed of fibrelass, resin and a catalyst formed under high heat and pressure. This new material helped produce panels that were smoother right out of the mold, resulting in higher-quality paint finishes. It was time to redesign the Gordon Keeble and Wayne Cherry was the man to do it.

He took some of his own '70s design cues and effectively produced the coolest coupe' of the era. Far more significantly here was proof that the design centre of excellence for General Motors in Europe had to be Luton. The Opel variants didn't look half as exciting as what was coming out of Bedfordshire at Motor Shows. Inadvertently then, taking a chance on a micro production, exclusive GT had the affect of actually increasing mass production of the new Cavalier and Viva and focusing attention on British based designers and engineers.

Meanwhile the Gordon Keeble went on in its own

uncomplicated and very simple way to remain the GT of choice. As Aston Martin limped from financial crisis to crisis and Jaguar didn't really have a model that was truly reliable, the Gordon Keeble was always there. A pretty car, that was light, powerful and wouldn't ever rust. Many reckoned it was the best Vauxhall related motor since the Prince Henry.

Autoreality: Gordon Keeble Dead Micro Brand

In May 1965, after building around 80 cars, Gordon-Keeble Ltd went into liquidation. However, Harold Smith, previously a Gordon-Keeble dealer, bought the manufacturing rights of the company.

Trading under the name of Keeble Cars Ltd, production of the Gordon-Keeble IT, as it was now known, continued for just over a year, enabling about 19 more cars to be made until the factory closed at the end of 1966.

Then in 1968, John de Bruyne from Newmarket in Suffolk announced the development of a revised version of the Gordon-Keeble, to be known as the de Bruyne which would be made the United States. Although a mid engined prototype was made and shown at the New York Motor Show, nothing more happened.

All car enthusiasts were left with was a supercar with the tortoise badge, not a turtle, apparently because one wandered into frame when being photographed for the original brochure. Still looks like a turtle to me...

14. Billy Rootes and the Hillman Beetles

Sir William (Billy) Rootes didn't particularly like what he saw. No one did, it was a factory in ruins. As the head of the appropriately named Rootes Commission he was unimpressed and recommended demolition, or "it will collapse of its own inertia within two years." The Commission also stated that, "the vehicle does not meet the fundamental technical requirements of a motor car. As regards performance and design it is quite unattractive to the average car buyer. It is too ugly and noisy." They concluded, "To build the car commercially would be a completely uneconomic enterprise." Rootes apparently addressed the Royal Engineers Major in charge of the factory with the words, "if you think you're going to build cars in this place, young man, you're a bloody fool."

On a bad day he may have left it right there and thought no more about it but Major Ivan Hirst was quite an impressive chap. Rallying his troops, a rag tag group of ex prisoners of war, and local workers to build something that actually worked. And anyway the Australians were after the plant and if they didn't take it the Russians would from just over the border. Rootes also heard that the Military Government of the Allied Zone needed twenty thousand cars ASAP.

"Major Hirst, I think you and I need to build a bigger and better factory together." Rootes wanted to establish more overseas plants and this was a great opportunity. Especially as there was twenty million marks available to supply those vehicles. Re-engineering the strange 'Beetle' to work better was doable and Hirst's 'can do' attitude was infectious.

The Major not only supervised production as it climbed rapidly, he also made some vital decisions. One was the retention of the pre-war V over W emblem and with it the adoption of the Volkswagen name. Rootes was overjoyed at having another marque badge to add to his collection. Not only that he managed to pull some strings and get Hirst honourably discharged from the army so he would be a full time employee. By the early 1950s production was going very well indeed, but Billy Rootes was very reluctant to import what had become known as the Beetle, to the UK. There was still a reluctance to consider German products. Anyway they could barely keep up with demand in Europe as Volkswagen got the continent on the move.

Back on home soil in 1955 two clever development engineers at Rootes were given a brief to look into the small car market. With a brief to come up with a vehicle that could do 60mph and 60mpg whilst carrying two adults and two children didn't go well. Shown the prototype at an early stage Rootes said, "Time to get the Germans involved."

A small engineering team from Wolfsburg went to Coventry. After a few weeks they had installed the Beetle's reliable air-cooled unit although the design of the saloon body was already very clean and modern. By 1957 it was ready to launch and Rootes reckoned that Germany would be a good place to launch what was a smaller, but more spacious Beetle.

The Volkswagen Imp was a massive success and it soon became Britain's most popular import, until Coventry took on some of the production for the UK market and it was rebadged as the Hillman Imp. It was now 1958 and BMC were seriously reconsidering whether to launch their own Mini as the Imp became the must have car.

The Imp brand could be stretched in the usual Rootes fashion with a faster Sunbeam model, better specification Singer and even an oddly luxurious Humber. Customers lapped them up. So BMC didn't bother with the mini and just looked on jealously as Hillman Beetles rolled out of Coventry and into the homes that had previously bought Morris Minors.

Ivan Hirst still ran the whole Volkswagen plant that had more than doubled in size, but as Sir Billy Rootes health

failed Hirst, was destined to take on responsibility for the whole group. He was instrumental in making sure that there was more to Volkswagen than the Beetle and Imp, updating them regularly. A range of larger rear engined Hillman Minx saloons began to challenge the Ford Cortina at the top of the UK bestseller charts in 1966 with 152,356 finding new homes. Oh, and in third place just behind the Cortina was the Austin 1100 another impressive showing for the Rootes Group. That's because the moribund BMC group was snapped up and in the process of being reshaped by Hirst and his team. The hatchback Imp was something of a sensation throughout the whole of Europe and even made deep inroads into the American sub compact market. They much preferred it to those funny Japanese things.

The Rootes Group export drive was continuous with manufacturing plants established around the world. Things weren't so great in the home market though. Union strife and increasing disruption saw the gradual migration of manufacturing to Germany and other Rootes plants in Europe. By 1975 the Neu Beetle and Hillman Minx were identical except for the badging.

When Hirst retired to become Life President of The Rootes Group in 1981 the entire British owned car industry was based in Europe. It took constant Government lobbying and incentives to bring limited Imp production back to Coventry. Meanwhile Wolseley and Riley were killed off in Europe but thrived in Japan along with the Humber, Sunbeam and Singer variants. Indeed a manufacturing plant was established in Nagoya to satisfy demand and local specifications.

By 1992 The Rootes Group had not just become the largest motor manufacturer in the world, but most significantly the most profitable, a situation that continues to this day with the Hybrid Hillman Minx range. Billy and his brother Reggie would be pleased to know that how their company operates what has been dubbed 'intelligent badge engineering'.

Autoreality: Ivan the hero & end of the Imp

It is possible to have a go at Volkswagen about a lot of things, but they have always acknowledged the part played by the Major Hirst.

Here's an extract from VW's own introduction to

their publication, Ivan Hirst British Officer and Manager of Volkswagen's Postwar Recovery: *Not only the actual survival of the Volkswagen Works in Wolfsburg after the Second World War, but also their present form can be largely accredited to the efforts of one Englishman: Ivan Hirst. The international press became interested in his life in February 2000 when he died at the age of 84. While 'The Guardian' commented, "Ivan Hirst. Englishman who made Volkswagen part of the German economic miracle the 'International Herald Tribune 'celebrated Hirst as the "rescuer of Volkswagen". 'The Times' described him as the "British soldier who got the Volkswagen Beetle on the road" And in the 'Automotive News' he was the "British officer who revived VW". None of these articles failed to underline the ironic twist of history: the decisive role in the reconstruction of the successful German automobile maker was played by a British officer."*

As for the Imp, it is a complicated and involved story and the massive amount of money needed to develop and build the Imp and the plant at Linwood are just a couple of the reasons why the Rootes Group collapsed and became involved with Chrysler Corporation.

Lord William Rootes set it up in 1964 as a partnership, but when he died that October control was slipping away. By 1967 the company had been acquired by Chrysler, to become part of Chrysler Europe.

Chrysler was blamed for the end of the Imp in March 1976, after fewer than 500,000 had been built. Mind you 9 years isn't a bad run for a poorly selling minicar. Two years later the Rootes Group became part of Peugeot. The Linwood plant closed in 1981. The Imp dream was over.

15. Jensen Bond

Ian Fleming imagined his hero James Bond in Casino Royale, behind the wheel of a 4.5 litre Bentley with an Amherst Villiers supercharger. It was a big brute of a car, which was Bond's personal, rather than his company transport. So when it came to making a film featuring James Bond it was inevitable that he should be seen in something rather more exciting than a creaky old vintage car.

Film producer Albert Broccoli started to cast around for car and in Dr. No ended up with the rather effeminate Sunbeam Alpine. For Goldfinger (1964) it had to be something that summed up the '60s and would really make it swing. It had to be a British car and a super stylish one too. Broccoli looked at Aston Martin, but thought that the car was a bit dated as the DB5 was only a mild update of the old DB4.

Then there was Bristol. It fitted well with the image of a gentleman about town, but it did seem less dashing than Broccoli had hoped for. It didn't help that part owner Tony Crook didn't like the idea of a Bristol being in a film at all. He reckoned it could bring all sorts of riff raff into his showroom.

What Broccoli really wanted was a Jaguar E-Type. The impact the model had around the world was incredible and fitted perfectly with James Bond's image. Apparently a call was put into Jaguar and the boss Sir William Lyons was put on the spot. Could the film crew borrow two? Lyons though was not keen. At the time the last thing he needed was more publicity for a car that he had trouble producing in large enough quantities anyway. Loaning two seemed stupid when he could sell them. Briefly Broccoli considered buying some secondhand E-Types and it was while his production crew was searching for those that they came across a Jensen.

You either love or loathe the look the Jensen CV8, but the film company could see all sorts of potential with this model. When approached by Broccoli directly the company were only too happy to help. Already the production designers were suggesting that the vehicle could be extensively modified especially as the script was going to reflect this with all sorts of stunts. Best of all, the fibreglass body meant that the modifications were quick and relatively easy to carry out. The quad headlamps hinged inwards to allow room for heavy calibre cannon and the side ejector seat worked a treat.

What the Bond production really liked was that Jensen had fairly advanced plans for new models. The P66 Interceptor may have been shown alongside the four-wheel drive FF at the 1965 Motor Show, but the film company already knew that an exciting new shape was coming. Already Jensen had drawings of the Vignale bodywork that was planned for the new range coming in the future. Meanwhile, the CV8 made an incredible impact in both Goldfinger in 1964 and Thunderball in 1965.

The real year of the Jensen Bond car was 1967 and You Only Live Twice. Although it was up against a flash Toyota, the all-new Interceptor had a real 'wow' factor. There were not many gadgets at all, but the Interceptor did not need any gimmicks. After all it helped Bond stop Blofeld in his tracks. The fact that a complete Autogyro could be incorporated into the glass rear hatch was a stroke of pure genius. This was the point at which the whole of America, well, the ones who could afford it anyway, wanted an Interceptor on their big drive.

Jensen became an Anglo American company with importer Kjell Qvale as it made sense to shift a lot of the production to the United States. Britain was becoming an increasingly difficult place to make cars and the availability of the Chrysler V8 was obviously much easier. A machine pressed body rather than a hand finished one was a major expense but it meant that sales targets could be met and profits were sky high. Indeed, it helped to finance some new smaller models.

Getting back to Bond, the Interceptor continued to be the secret agent's go to car. Diamonds Are Forever (1971) may have been full of American cars but that now half included Jensen. Flushed with cash the company could finance a new model, which they called the Esporanda.

Designed by William Townes it was a wonderfully wedgey creation. Although it wasn't ready for The Man with the Golden Gun in 1974 by the time of The Spy Who Loved Me was released in 1977, it had a starring underwater role.

With Jensen as one of the largest manufacturers of sports cars in the world whilst Bristol and Aston Martin are now obsolete marques, it is impossible to think of Bond behind the wheel of any other car.

Autoreality: FFFantastic Jensen

Huge thanks to GKN for letting me reproduce this brochure image reproduced here. What a remarkable creation it was. The facts are that on a rainy day in September 1972, GKN's Hemi-powered four-wheel-drive FFF 100 created a new world record at the MIRA test track with drag racer Dennis Priddle behind the wheel.

It accelerated from a standing start, up to 100 mph, and back to a stop in just 12.2. seconds. Eight seconds less than the world record at that time, and a record that remained unbroken until 2004.

GKN, a motor industry titan, who developed the CV joints which made the mini the front wheel drive legend it became, had a forward thinking managing director, Claude Birch. He had purchased a four-wheel-drive Jensen FF direct from Jensen Motors, and was impressed by the engineering.

In 1971, the same year that the FF would be discontinued, Birch came up with the idea of producing a one off experimental car based on the FF and fitted with the powerful Chrysler 426 'Hemi' engine.

Named the FFF 100, it would have full race specification, and using the road holding and braking abilities of the Ferguson four-wheel-drive system and Maxaret anti-lock braking to test the performance and durability of some of GKN's specialised components. Here was a brilliant promotional tool and be painted in blue and white GKN colours.

Jensen Motors sold GKN an FF chassis, which was stiffened. The overall weight of the FFF 100 would be lighter than the Jensen FF, so softer springs were fitted to the front suspension, and less spring leaves were used to the rear to give the correct ride height.

Ventilated disc brakes were fitted with special hubs, allowing big Kent Alloy aluminium wheels to be fitted, along

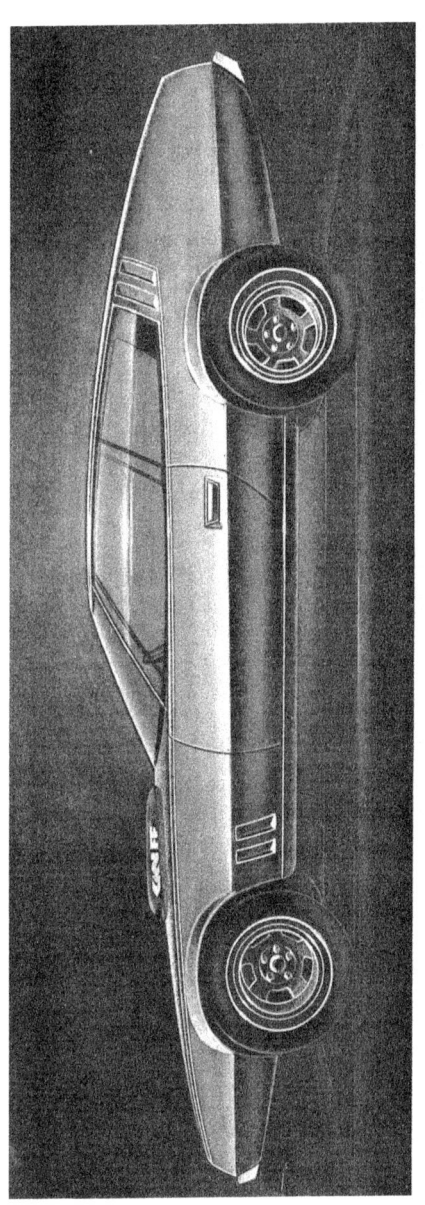

FFF 100

FERGUSON FORMULA FOUR-WHEEL-DRIVE TEST CAR

with a modified Adwest steering rack and the power assistance removed.

Chrysler's 426 'Hemi' engine produced 600bhp being was based on a A990 drag racing engine with dry sump lubrication. Inside there was NASCAR TRW pistons, solid lifter tappets and an STX 24 camshaft with a compression ratio of 11.5:1 and the finished engine with twin Holley carburettors.

The car still exists and was on the classic car show circuit in America and more recently in the UK. I'm quite happy to buy it if the current owner is a bit bored by its uniqueness.

THE JENSEN FF.

16. The Ledwinka Lancias

The Tatra story started in a Moravian village called Nesseldorf in the mid 19th century, a carpentry company producing carts and coaches but later moved into rolling stock and from 1897 cars. The car company was called Nesseldorf. However, the arrival of Austrian Hans Ledwinka a very talented engineer who had two stints with the company, transformed its products.

Renamed Tatra in 1923 after the mountains in which the vehicles were tested, Ledwinka's brilliant idea was to build cars and trucks in an identical manner. He did away with a conventional frame but utilised a large diameter central tube with the power unit at one end and the coachwork supported by it. The resulting Tatra T.11 was light, cheap to buy and comfortable, but the air-cooled engine was noisy and was soon nicknamed Tatra-tra-tra-tra.

Then In 1933 Ledwinka designed the T.570 an economy car with a rear mounted air-cooled engine, independent suspension and a sloping body. It could almost be described as looking rather Beetleish. Indeed, it preceded the Doctor Ferdinand Porsche designed Type 60, which was a hotchpotch of 1930s technology, which effectively borrowed the streamlined styling, and engineering technology from the Czech built Tatras. Ledwinka started legal proceedings, but the war got in the way. Indeed he saw his patents confiscated and ultimately he was accused of colluding with the enemy and sentenced to six years in prison. Meanwhile Tatra was nationalised by the Communist Government and the company went back to building trucks and trains, briefly making the streamlined T.77 model purely for party officials.

Hans Ledwinka, had plenty of time to think about what to do next and draw up plans for a fresh car. He had no intention of returning to Austria. He felt as though he had been forced out of work by Mercedes, Volkswagen and BMW. So he travelled to where he believed there were kindred engineering spirits. Italy. Specifically Lancia.

Ledwinka had plans to revive the T.570, but this time with a decent engine. What Italy and indeed the rest of the world really needed was a family car with rather more practicality than the Beetle, or even a Fiat 500 offered. Lancia were happy to take the Austrian on board not least because their advanced engineering was all very well, but they needed a mass market not just to survive, but also to prosper.

The 'Lewinka Lancias' as they were dubbed became a revelation. He took the Appia and gave it a more practical twist. Itself a downmarket version of the Aurelia, the suicide doors were all very well but expensive to engineer, better to spend that money reinforcing the body and making the rear boot into a tailgate. Also using aluminium panels seemed like an extravagance, so the bodywork was entirely pressed steel. Aware of the poor reputation of Italian cars to disintegrate outside of the home climate, he insisted on galvanising the floor pans and inner wings. Ledwinka wanted to turn the model into an affordable and practical car. The Lancia Persone (which sounded stranger in Italian than anywhere else) was born with an eager and space saving V4 engine. Here was a true people's car that had an appeal far outside of its home country.

In many ways the Lancia Persone was the perfect combination of the Morris Minor and a Volkswagen Beetle, but with a charismatic Italian twist. Not only did it become a best seller in Italy, Europe could see the benefit of having such a practical car. Best of all America took to the Persone in the way it had never embraced any Italian car. Launched in 1956, by 1959 it was the best selling car in Europe and the top import in America.

Lewinka soon had the finance to change the Persone more radically than ever. He was always impressed by the Citroen Traction Avant and could see the way the

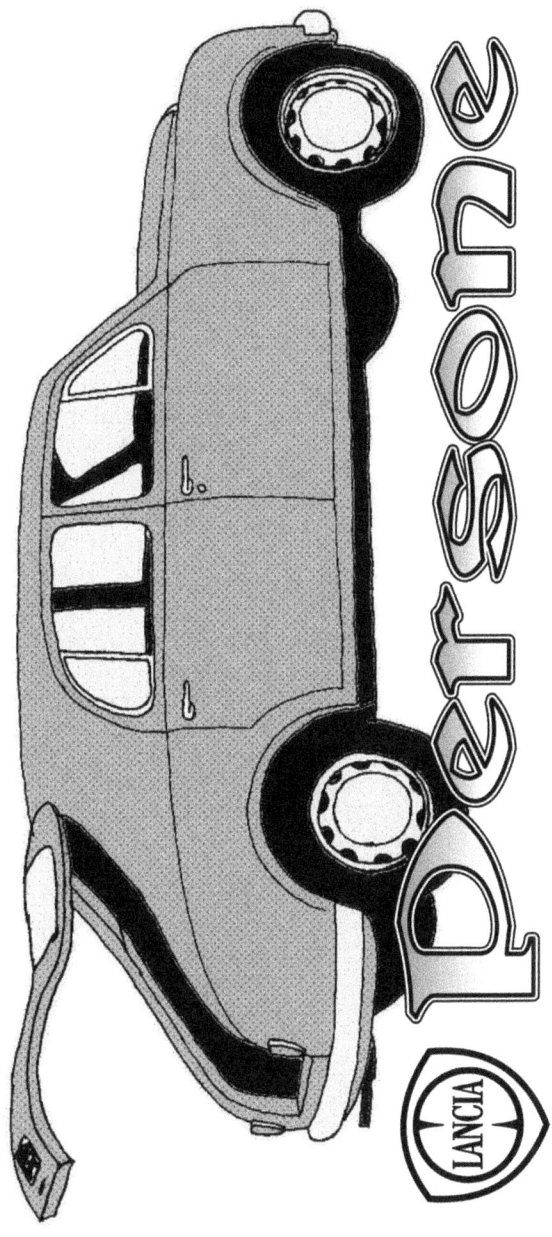

automotive world would be moving with the Austin Morris Mini. Even though the Mini struggled initially the space saving and handling benefits of the new breed of small car had a massive appeal to the engineer who was always thinking of the future.

Ledwinka died in 1967 but not before the Persone had been completely revamped as a front wheel drive proto-multi purpose vehicle that really did become the people's choice worldwide. Perhaps the most significant result of the Ledwinka Lancias is that they effectively financed the upmarket Flavia and sporting Fulvia models so that they were better built and more desirable than they had ever been. It also funded their increasingly successful racing programme.

For many it was no surprise in 1969 when Lancia bought the ailing and debt ridden Fiat car division for a token few Lira and just a few years later in 1971 the moribund Volkswagen company that had failed to better the Beetle shut down. Lewinka would have been proud and pleased that justice had finally been done.

Autoreality: Tatra Road Lorries

After the war, occupied Czechslovakia built Tata limousines for the Communist Party whilst concentrating on making lorries. The main car was the Tatra 600 called the Tatraplan from 1948. Then there was the three headlamped 603 from 1956. Still the preserve of the party officials and factory managers rather than the people. Some were exported. From 1975 it was the less rounded 613 and finally the post communist era 700 from 1996, which had an air cooled V8 and there was even a two door coupe.

Mostly it was all about the lorries which are super tough with their 4, 6 or 8 wheel-drive transmission systems and incredible off road ability Tatra's lorries won six Paris Dakar victories in the Auto-Camion category.

No more Tatra cars then. Meanwhile it is a questionable whether good old Lancia will survive after years of mismanagement and misguided badge chicanary. We won't dwell on that.

17. MG Landcrab Love

BMC ADO17, the Austin Design Office nomenclature announced the arrival of the British Motor Corporation's (BMC) first hatchback. Produced from September 1964 to 1975 and sold first of all as the Austin 1600. It was the large part of the small (mini), medium (Austin/Morris 1100-1300) front wheel drive model line up that transformed the company.

It could have been prettier and was also referred to as the "Landcrab", but it could not have been more practical and it was tough as the crustaceans it was nick named after. The 1622cc B Series engine was more than adequate to pull it along and the handling was secure, fun and stable. Hardly surprising that the 1600 was voted European Car of the Year for 1965.

Alec Issigonis and Pininfarina designed the exterior and it was truly inspired to incorporate the large rear hatchback. Issigonis had his finger on the pulse of designers in Europe who were moving towards a three and five door layout. Despite that the bodyshell was incredibly rigid which only enhanced its reputation for toughness, which came in handy when it went rallying.

The 1600 was spacious, with great visibility and a throughly modern minimalist interior much like the 1100-1300 with a similar instrument display with ribbon speedometer and green indicator light on the end of the indicator stalk. There was a chrome umbrella style handbrake under the dashboard parcel shelf. The latest BMC technology was well to the fore with Hydrolastic suspension and a clever brake bias system between the front and rear wheels.

Although it started life as an Austin it was soon sold as the Morris 1600 and Wolseley 1600 in 1966 and 1967, which catered for the wide variety of marques sold by the BMC dealerships. Although there were constant updates that changed the suspension set up, steering, seats and heating controls to name just a few. Technically they were constantly tinkering to get it right.

The biggest changes came in 1968 with the arrival of the Mark II. Overall it made the model slightly more conventional on the inside, simplified the styling overall making things a bit cheaper and more affordable The slim, horizontal rear lights were replaced by vertical ones which meant that the tailgate lip was done away with and the boot would now open right down to the bumper. Although the compression ratio was increased, the most significant innovation was bringing in yet another badge to boost the ADO17 range, the famous MG octagon.

Here was the MG ZT Sportbrake. On the outside the theme was matt black with a standard vinyl roof, which could be deleted, 14 inch Rostyle alloys and black detailing around the lights. Extra spots were included. Instead of hydrolastic suspension, there was a larger, beefed up version of the mini's classic dry rubber system.

Inside there was lots of crackle finish on the dashboard and a Mota Lita sports steering wheel, vinyl bucket seats with competition style four point seat belts and a 130 mph speedometer. Under the bonnet, the 1800 engine was persuaded to deliver 100bhp and it had twin SU HS6 carburetors.

Meanwhile, for those that needed it Special Vehicle Operations (SVO) offered a stripped out competition ready model with a roll cage, performance and preparation options. This was in response to the MG version in particular becoming the star of so many endurance events. Winning the 1968 London-Sydney Marathon and then taking the top three spots at the 1970 London to Mexico World Cup Rally was a phenomenal result. The Paris Dakar was the next challenge and the MG dominated that race in the early '70s.

What no one saw coming was the MG Sportbrake V8. Putting the Buick engine into the Landcrab created one

hell of a beast. It was marketed as a performance saloon, rather than the comfy old Rover option. Arriving in 1971 it thrived until the fuel crisis pegged sales back a bit. There were some concessions to luxury with an optional dab of leather and wood trim if required.

However, BMC now had a decent revenue stream from their three very popular models so they could revel in their independence whilst other companies around them struggled, merged and failed. It was important hough to shorten the model cycle and ten years was becoming far too long.

The replacement in 1975 was the wedge shaped Austin Morris 1600 with no Wolseley model, but the popular MG variant continued. There was no buyer resistance at all. The original 1600 had won over a lot of customers with its reliability and practicality. The mostly new wedge looked like it was ready for the 1970s and the hatchback bodywork had never been more relevant. Another best seller for BMC.

Autoreality: Landcrab is dead...Long live the Wedge

We have been really quite unecessarily overkind to the 1800, but it was worth doing to blot out the bad times. Certainly it did have some success such as finishing second in the 1968 London-Sydney Marathon and taking three of the top 20 positions competing in the 1970 London to Mexico World Cup Rally.

There were some fundamental cock ups with the 1800, not least that the dipstick markings were wrong on the 1964 models. Obviously it wasn't a looker, surprising as Pininfarina were involved, but they were just cleaning up what the BMC team (Issigonis) had created. It could have been more desirable to look at, but again that was the least of its problems.

For a start It could have had a more appropriate engine, which was too large and thirsty for the average family car buyer. It was also a bit too huge inside, possibly too large as potential buyers did not know what to do with all that space. It confused them. Mostly though all that extra engine and space made it significantly more expensive than rival family cars.

What really killed the ADO17, although it took 11 years to happen, was a lack of sales. It had been predicted that 200,000 a year would go through BMC showrooms. Instead 40,000 was the peak and by the end a risible 20,000 of all types found new homes. The public had spoken and it also hastened Issigonis retirement from the company, although he still beavered away at home on designing future automotive products. It could have been his brilliant swanswong, instead is was a crabby failure.

18. The Real Italian Job

Many believed that it was Innocenti who saved the Mini. Issigonis may have designed it, but the Italian company had a big hand in its survival, revival and the development of a bigger better organisation that would thrive away from British Leyland.

Founded by Ferdinand Innocenti in 1933 the company was better know for manufacture of the mod's other favourite motor scooter in the shape of the Lambretta. However, Innocenti was ambitious when in 1960 it began production of licence built Austin A40s that initiated a long association with the British company which included the Austin/Morris 1100. They also reproduced the Austin Healey Sprite and beautifully rebodied it with coupe' styling by Osi and a convertible by Ghia, production ran for ten years from 1960. So if they could tackle that legendary British sports car, they could certainly take on the Mini and win.

With the passing of Ferdinand Innocenti in 1972, BL stepped in to what was the biggest overseas market for Minis and set up a new company which was called Leyland Innocenti SpA. The new boss was Geoffrey Robinson and the whole range was renamed. The quaint Mini Minor, became the much more mundane Mini 1000 and an upmarket 1001 which had a timber finish on the instrument binnacle and a 51 bhp engine. The Mini-Matic retained its name, whilst the estate got an upper case t to become the 1000T. A new Mini Cooper 1300 came with UK Cooper S power and was an important revival of a charismatic name for the simple reason that the company never signed the same agreement as BMC to end paying John Cooper a royalty. In 1974 though everything changed as the shape of Minis became fashionably rectangular.

The Mini 90 and 120 was the first official hatchback based Mini. Styled by Bertone it was a contemporary square cut design and was arguably one of the first Euro superminis. Underneath it all of course was standard A series Mini running gear yet it was only marginally larger than the old car being just 2.6 in longer and 3.5in wider. The Mini 90 had the 998cc engine producing 49bhp which translated into a 87mph top speed and was distinguished by its black bumpers. The 120 had a detuned 65 bhp 1275cc unit with twin carburettors which would reach 96 mph and revelled in chrome bumpers. The only mechanical changes were a repositioned radiator now mounted at the front and a revised exhaust. Inside, the rear seat folded forward and despite a high loading lip, offered a usefully large luggage area. The most distinctive part of the interior was the dashboard which echoed the original Mini's central pod, though only a stylised Mini logo occupied this space whilst in front of the driver though were rectangular cut outs.

Robinson was so excited by the model that he managed to not only enthuse BL management back home, he convinced them to make more funds available to what was then a struggling concern. That's because they now wanted to bring the Italian Mini to Blighty. It wasn't much of a stretch as most of the mechanical components and some of the body pressings originated in Britain anyway. To pay for it they cancelled the prototype ADO88 on the grounds that it would be pointless to have yet another small hatchback.

British Leyland launched the Mini Italia in late 1975. It was an instant hit. The huge number of orders that the dealers were getting put a lot of pressure on the government who agreed to bankroll production in Britain and the unions who could see that they might just have a job for life. Perhaps the cleverest thing was that Robinson had commissioned a four door Mini Italia. This was effectively a real replacement for the best selling 1100/1300 range. Meanwhile the British buying public were ignoring the Italian named Allegro in favour of the Italia 1100/1300. So the Allegro was allowed to quickly die whilst the Italia flourished not just in the home market, and Italy, where it wasn't called the Italia at all, but throughout Europe and Japan the Mini 90, 110 and 120. It was a clear best seller.

Obviously the build quality was a bit iffy for a while, but despite these setbacks the appeal was universal. The arrival of Sir Michael Edwardes led to the Mini Italia becoming a stand alone company which he spun off to go it alone outside of the Rover Group. A good job too as BL would eventually go bankrupt in the early '90s whilst Mini Italias in the UK and Mini 90/110/120 worldwide remains the most innovative and largest premium small car brand worldwide.

Autoreality: Nottacenti in the UK

Of course the big debate back in 1975 when cars were tested in the UK was, 'Will it ever come to Britain?' Leyland seriously considered the possibility, especially as most of the mechanical components and some of the body pressings originated in Britain. Plans were drawn up for a limited run of 5,000, but BL pulled out. Production costs on this car proved to be very high and anyway the prototype ADO88 was well under way at that time and would eventually metamorphose into the Metro. In fact, it may be a good thing that the Innocenti never came here officially. That's because all the models, which were imported unofficially, seemed to fall apart and then rust to bits in a very short time. Something to do with low grade Eastern Block steel and Italian build quality. As if Leyland's troubles weren't bad enough, adding an Italian built car to the range could have finished them off much sooner.

In fact BL's financial woes were not unconnected with Innocenti's bankruptcy in 1975. Fiat were interested in buying the company, but De Tomaso beat them to it. The standard Mini was discontinued although Cooper production staggered into '76 thanks to factory left overs. De Tomaso had plans, and this included the Mini De Tomaso based on a 120, but with a 74bhp engine. It was effectively a very welcome mid '70s Cooper S and headed a three car range that comprised the 90, 120 and De Tomaso. In 1982 the A series power plant was replaced by a three cylinder Daihatsu unit to make the Mini 3. That car became the Innocenti Small and in 1990 Fiat finally got their hands on the company. In 1993 the car was discontinued.

I was contacted by a reader Anthony Marfleet a few years back who told me about his '70s encounter with an Innocenti, "I was the local Area Manager – (posh for salesman) circa 1974/5 in the SW London area where

Goodyear had a depot in the Balham High Road. One day I turned up and saw the Service Manager, Fred attending to the wheel rims of the Chairman of BLMC, Sir Donald - later Lord Stokes' - Innocenti Mini - I say "attending" as he was actually "roughing up" the bead seats all around the shiny new rims with a file!

"Apparently the tubed 155/70S12 Goodyear G800+S Supersteel tyres were slipping round the rims and in danger of forcing the valves be squashed out of the wheels. Fred was quite adept at sorting out such problems and asked me if I'd like to take the car around the block to see if his brainwave had cured the problem. I jumped at the chance and returned after a circuitous route of Balham and we found no slippage at all. Luckily nobody was any the wiser until, maybe, the tyres were replaced!

"I wondered then why BLMC hadn't taken on this car as a very adequate replacement for the then Mini as it would have been a good seller in the UK."

19. Horseless Gas Carriage

James Watt did not invent the steam engine, but he did make it work. Watt had the brilliant idea of condensing the steam in a separate vessel, which removed the need for heating and cooling. This made the engine faster, safer, and more fuel-efficient. In 1774 he joined Matthew Boulton, Birmingham's leading manufacturer, in order to market his invention, a partnership that has become one of the most famous in history. Working for both of them was William Murdoch.

The son of an Ayrshire mill designer, he was a brilliant natural mechanic and, in 1777, walked 300 miles to Birmingham to meet Watt. Along with business partner, Boulton, they took him on and he soon became works manager. Murdoch also conducted his own research into making steam engines better by making them smaller and able to operate at much higher pressure. His employers were not at all keen.

Murdoch moved to Redruth in Cornwall to install mine engines and he took the opportunity to indulge in his passion for making steam engines do new and exciting things. There in 1786 he built a three-wheeled contraption and fitted one of his compact high pressure engines to drive the rear wheels. Famously he did some late night research and development. One night spitting fire, belching smoke and making one hell of a racket he scared the living daylights out of a clergyman. Convinced it was the devil he ran as fast as he could away from the steam vehicle.

Although some locals were terrified, others were inspired. A young Richard Trevithick in particular paid close attention to this new local hero. As Murdoch continued to develop his small engines, Trevithick was thinking much bigger. This culminated in the 'Puffing Devil', the first passenger-carrying vehicle powered by steam, made its debut on a road outside Redruth in Cornwall on December 24th, 1801. The trouble was this engine could only run for very short distances unable to maintain constant pressure.

Murdoch learned of the Puffing Devil and he decided that it was time to go it alone in the steam business. He knew that his designs were better and he was more than ready to introduce a new mode of transport. The Murdoch Steam Carriage Company Limited was incorporated and he quickly found a lot of wealthy investors, none of whom were called Watt or Boulton.

Whereas the majority of horseless steam carriages would be large passenger carrying beasts like those designed by Sir Goldsworthy Gurney in the 1820s, Murdoch was determined to keep his carriages compact. He knew that it was difficult to persuade passengers to climb aboard a vehicle that was uncomfortable and not very manoeuvrable. What also worked against them was the lack of sophisticated road surfaces that meant wheels would be prone to break up and the carriage break down.

Murdoch's small, powerful steam engine would heat up quickly burn cleanly for an hour enabling the driver to cover an impressive twenty or more miles an hour depending on the road conditions. The wheels were large so that they could soak up any road imperfections more easily. The bodywork was set low, but with a decent amount of ground clearance and steering was by a rods. Murdoch was convinced that keeping the number of passengers to a maximum of three plus the driver was the key. Small nimble vehicles were the key to their success. Officially they were called Murdoch Mobiles, but to the people in the street who often had to jump out of their way, these were 'Boilers'.

Murdoch could see the limitations of steam power and the amount of energy and botheration required to keep the coal or wood fire burning. However, he was already

AutoFutropolis – Car History Rebooted

This truly remarkable personal conveyance - Murdoch Mobile runs on the purest gases. Refills are not not required for many days if used under normal circumstances. No licences are needed to operate the Mobile and there are no age restrictions and it is perfectly acceptable for a gentlewoman to use. Gas lights are available at extra cost from your local concessionaire.

Murdoch Gas & Steam Carriage Company Limited

thinking well ahead as he had already begun to experiment with coal gas to create lighting. Bottling the gas and creating a nationwide network of refilling stations was something that the Victorian business owners could really get behind. Murdoch mobiles were never cheap but they became incredibly popular with the growing middle class and helped to kick start Victoria's reign in 1837 and spread British influence around the world almost as fast as the railways. Trains were for the masses, but the Murdoch Mobiles were for those who could afford to show off.

Murdoch passed away in 1839, but his invention was constantly developed by his huge company. It was even adopted by the military who favoured the autonomous approach to warfare and these were christened Autonobombs.

The Mobiles largely brought prosperity, peace and obviously mobility to City centres around the world. Whether they were used by private owners or as taxis the gas, be it LPG, CNG or methane, burned cleanly and relatively cheaply. Although there are competing companies making similar vehicles almost everyone still refers to their 'Murdoch' and just a few still call them 'Boilers.'

Autoreality: Murdoch Switches the Lights On

William Murdoch deserves to be much better known for his quite incredible achievements. In 1792 Murdoch was the first person in the world to light his house and office by piped coal gas. Shame he is not around today to fix the gas crisis. He also invented a process for clearing beer. In 1817 Murdoch built a large house outside Birmingham and it incorporated his own system of gas lighting, a doorbell worked by compressed air and a rather clever stove based air conditioning system. And of course there is his road locomotive.

There are precious few details, but in 2000 the Murdoch Flyer Project began to recreate this historic vehicle in Redruth. The locomotive design is based on Murdoch`s model steam carriage of 1784 and other information resulting from research carried out by members. The full-size working replica was constructed by project members between 2004 and 2007. It has been on static display, and occasionally all steamed up, at selected Cornish steam rallies and in Redruth on Murdoch Day.

The Murdoch Flyer is now located at the Moseley Toy and Train Museum. Pay a visit, I certainly plan to.

20. When Mercedes bought NSU

NSU had a complicated history, best known for making motorcycles and mopeds until 1957 when they dived back into the car market with the rear engined NSU Prinz. Here was a small car, much like a German Hillman Imp in style and execution which sold in decent numbers, but then in 1967 they got a bit too ambitious.

Without doubt, the NSU Ro80 was a technical tour de force when it was launched in 1967 and crowned 'Car of the Year' for 1968. Not only did it have a Rotary engine, it was helped along by a semi-automatic three-speed transmission. Press a button on top of the lever and it changed gears via a vacuum system without the hassle of pressing a clutch. Steering was easy because it was powered by the engine, plus it was pulled along by front wheel drive at a time when this was a rarity on larger cars. The long travel strut suspension meant that it had a very smooth ride with disc brakes all around to keep drivers out of trouble. It really did look like it had been sent from the future but not in a negative Terminator sort of way, until that is, buyers started using them, at which point the Ro80 terminated itself rather too easily.

Drivers knew they were in trouble when at first the car would seem sluggish, then the fuel consumption would shoot up and there would be rather a lot of smoke. Finally, when the engine became reluctant to start the owner would take it to the garage where the service manager would have to draw a lot of air through his teeth, shake his head a lot and start filling in warranty claim forms. Early cars used carbon seals, which wore out quickly, sometimes after just 15,000 miles. NSU then switched to cast iron based material, which was technically known as IKA in 1969. The trouble was that this new material proved to be too brittle so that the seal edges would chip and break up.

NSU were in serious financial difficulties and the rumour was that Volkswagen was poised to take them over. Daimler-Benz swooped in and bought them up in 1969. They always regretted selling Auto Union to VW and anyway they had a plan for making NSU's rotary better. Back in 1961 Mercedes took out a licence to make the Wankel rotary engine. There were three rotors, which in conventional engine terms amounted to a size of 3.6 litres and sending its power through a five-speed transaxle. They were all ready to reveal their fully working concept C111. Instead of wearing a Mercedes three-pointed star, large NSU badges were glued on.

Their Wankel was carefully positioned in the middle of the car. It was surrounded by a wind cheating, lightweight glass fibre bodywork, which was bonded and riveted to a combined steel frame and floor unit. It produced stunning statistics, a top speed of over 160mph and it would get to 60mph in around 5 seconds, comfortably quicker than anything other than a fully prepared racing car. Indeed, this was no one off and Mercedes had produced an upgraded C111 within six months, which had more aerodynamic bodywork with improved all round visibility. Significantly it added yet another rotor to the engine which was now the equivalent of 4.8 litres in size which made it even quicker.

So what Mercedes were up was creating a new high technology brand. Mercedes realised that their customers were not going to accept wild and wacky ideas and concepts with their badge on it. NSU although slightly associated with failure created an opportunity to show off what their engineers could do. The first thing was to make the Ro80 not break down which they did by using Ferotic on the rotor tips, which was an Iron and titanium compound.

Secondly, NSU had a conventionally engined saloon ready to be launched. Mercedes decided to go ahead with the C70 with a plan and fit their 2.0 litre units as a sort of entry level Merc, but with a slightly more sporting twist.

Thirdly it was spinning off the C111 into it's own unique gull winged model range. First of all the NSU Wankel supercar established what they were all about. Then after some drastic reengineering a four seat front engined C111 was introduced as a long distance luxury supercar. In 1976

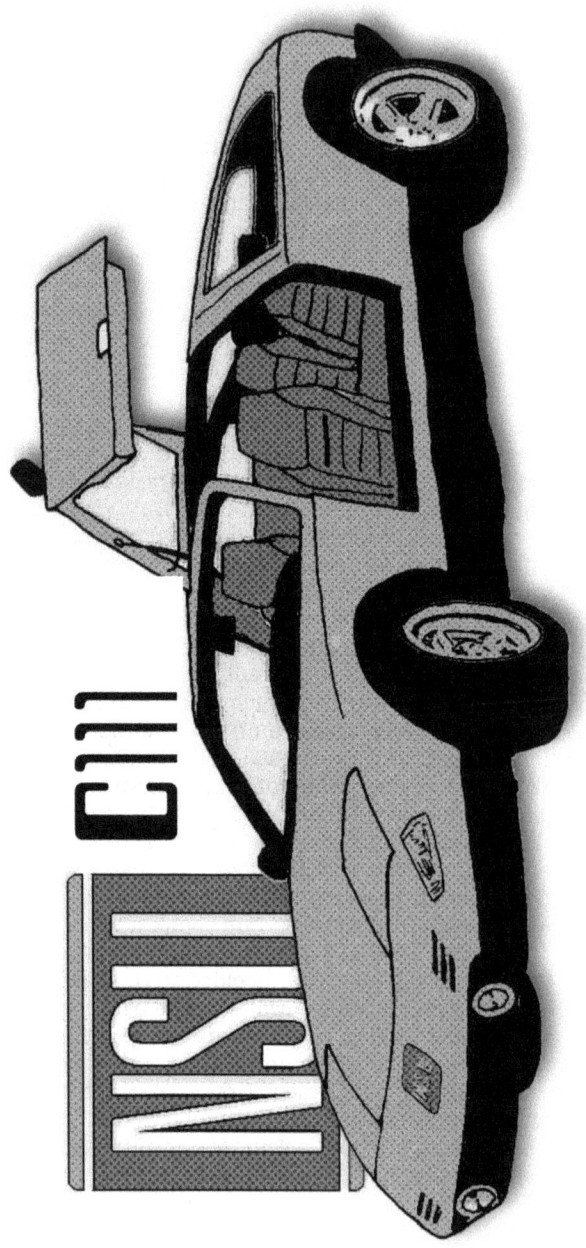

it was used as the sexy bodywork for the company's new 5 cylinder diesel engine and tuned to 190bhp it did some record breaking runs at the Nardo test track in Italy. Putting a diesel engine in anything but a taxi would have been viewed as highly eccentric. In the 21st century it could be seen as highly prescient. Yes the C111 was ahead of its time in using alternative propulsion and fuel systems.

NSU remains the high technology leader in the motor industry. They are celebrating ten years of hydrogen power across their range from the city C30, the family sized C70, the executive C80 and the supercar C111.

Autoreality: Wankel Reality

What actually happened was very simple. Volkswagen were the first to pick up the pieces of NSU. Taken over in 1969 the new, merged, company was called Audi NSU Auto Union AG. This incorporated the NSU and DKW marques into one and explains the four interlocking rings of Auto Union. The management of the Neckarsulm NSU plant moved to Audi's headquarters in Ingolstadt. The rear engined NSU models, Prinz 4, 1000 and 1200 were discontinued in 1973 and the Ro 80 was the last NSU badged car still in production.

Then there was Mercedes-Benz C111 in September

1969, a supercar with gullwing doors and a Wankel rotary engine. It was a research vehicle and one of the objectives was to test the use of glass-fibre-reinforced plastic for automotive bodyshells. The car was, in addition, to be used for the testing of the rotary piston engine, which sadly did not have a future. Fuel economy was not spectacular, but this was a 200mph supercar, but it was stringent emission regulations that were being implemented in the USA that killed off the C111.

It did however refuse to die. The test department fitted the C 111-II with a three-litre five-cylinder diesel engine. Now known internally as the C 111-II D, the test vehicle used turbocharging and intercooling systems to produce 190 bhp from standard 240D engine. In June 1976 the C 111 went to the test circuit at Nardò in Italy and over 60 hours, with four drivers set 16 world records, among them 13 for diesel vehicles and three for cars with any type of engine. The average speed was 156mph.

The C111 would not sit quietly in a museum because in 2011 GWA Tuning drafted a one-off prototype based on the Mercedes-Benz C111 called the Ciento Once. The proposal included a tubular space frame chassis with a Mercedes M120 V12 engine producing 408 bhp. Nice idea but no one made or bought any.

21. Those Bargain Renault Porsches

Ferdinand Porsche encountered some personal difficulties when the Second World War ended. Although he had never joined the Nazi Party slave workers were certainly used in the factories that made the military projects he was involved with. For a short while Porsche was able to get on with his old life. Safely relocated to rural Gmund in Austria, he just tackled engineering projects that came up in Stuttgart and Wolfsburg. So imagine his delight when the French Army invited him to tea at their military headquarters in Baden Baden near Stuttgart. All they wanted to know was whether he would be interested in making a less German version of the Beetle for Renault and calling it the 4CV.

However, it all went pear shaped very quickly as Porsche was denounced as a war criminal and imprisoned along with his son Ferry and brother-in-law Anton Piech. The allegation was that French nationals had been forced to work in the Volkswagen plant. Ferry Porsche was released, but his father wasn't, effectively being held to ransom although he was never charged with any crime. So Ferry set about restablishing the company, designing a four wheel drive grand prix car for Cisitalia in Italy and generated enough money to post bail for his father and Piech. Porsche the car company was back in business. It was now 1947.

However, Ferdinand had to sign some documentation and jot down some model proposals before he could be released. Indeed, despite never facing any sort of trial, he had plenty of time to sketch ideas having spent twenty months in a Dijon jail. Renault were interested in the sporting side of things and that was an area where Porsche had some form. He had not just proposed a sports car based on the Beetle he even built three Volkswagen Type 64s in 1939 specifically to compete in a fascist dictatorship capital to capital competition, also known as the Berlin-Rome race. Postponed, due to hostilities the cars were streamlined vehicles with all the wheels shrouded and a classic teardrop shape. Despite the VW badge these were effectively the first Porsches. Renault wondered whether they might make a more performance orientated Renault, or Renorsche.

Yes one of the bits of paper Porsche had signed in order to gain his release was the authorisation to use this concocted name to allow Renault to produce sporting versions of their own vehicles and also a sports marque related to any future vehices that Porsche might be involved with.

Well the former, Porsche couldn't do much about, but the latter was something he chose to completely ignore and when time allowed he would engage in legal action.

Renault kept an eye on what the Porsche engineering consultancy were doing and when the 356 came out, just a short while after so did the Renorsche R1052 Sport. In effect the Renorches were less expensive Porkers that were not quite so rigorously engineered, but they quickly gained a strong following as the rear, engined, rear wheel drive 4CV became the basis for these models. Privateer racers could adapt and modify easily enough and private buyers were happy to buy anything that was interesting in those dull post war days.

Porsche was too busy establishing themselves to be too concerned about the Renorsches. It was an irritant, but something that they could live with. However matters reached something of a head in the middle '60s when the Renorsche version of the 911, the R1255 broke cover. It was underpowered, but looked 911 enough to begin to confuse retail buyers and bring into question what Porsche actually stood for. Indeed Porsche managed to strong arm Renorsche out of various markets by insisting that they would no longer export to that territory if the French version was sold there. There were no Renorche dealerships in Germany, or Austria, or the United States. The UK was a different and both marques had their loyal followers. Profits for Renault though were starting to tail off.

When the fuel crisis hit in the early 1970s being in the low mpg sports car business seemed like a stupid thing

AutoFutropolis – Car History Rebooted

to do and anyway Alpine was now Renault's go to sports brand. Renault, as a state owned company did the unthinkable and actually sold of the Renorche company which included the factory in a management buy out in 1975. They got some cash and off loaded what had become a loss making side of their business. The newly independent company struggled and welcomed a fresh cash injection, even if that meant giving up control. Big mistake.

The investors were the Porsche board who twenty years later were taking their revenge. They acted swiftly and shut down the factory, smashed up the completed and uncompleted cars and bulldozed the factory into the ground. Then it was turned into an industrial estate. They would make it their mission to destroy any Renorches they came across.

You can't blame them as it seemed bonkers to allow a pseudo Porsche company to exist at all, but if you have a Renorsche in your garage right now it could well be priceless.

Autoreality: Porsche, The War Years...

In 2017 "Porsche: Vom Konstruktionsbüro zur Weltmarke" ("Porsche: From Engineering office to Global Brand") by historian Wolfram Pyta tells the story of Porsche GmbH/KG in the early years: from the origins of the Volkswagen to the transition to a wartime economy under National Socialism (Nazis) and the development of battle tanks, right up to the creation of the automotive brand called Porsche.

Professor Ferdinand Porsche success is closely linked to the "Third Reich" and Adolf Hitler himself from the Auto Union racing cars to the 'Strength through Joy' Volkswagen. Like most German companies during the Second World War, Dr. Ing. h.c. F. Porsche KG, as it was then known, exploited a labour force made up of foreign workers who were forced into service.

Pyta reckons that his own collaboration was not based on sharing the ideology with Hitler and his gang, but economically. He wanted to protect his family business, even though he was turning a blind eye to some terrible events. Porsche KG employed more than 400 forced labourers. Apparently the company was more lenient in the treatment of its workforce than the Volkswagen plant, which was nice of him.

When it came to his imprisonment after the war, Porsche was not convicted as a war criminal, incredibly it was simply Renault and Peugeot arguing over Porsche's role in the possible development of their own people's Beetle. He certainly provided technical advice. It was not until July 1947 that Porsche was released from custody on bail. He was acquitted in May 1948. Meanwhile Louis Renault was influenced enough by the Beetle to engineer a rear mounted four cylinder engine in the 4CV.

22. When Rolls were really Jags

Ironically what brought down Rolls-Royce was the aircraft. Chairman Sir Denning Pearson was determined to penetrate the important American market, but the competition from Pratt & Whitney and General Electric was overwhelming. Meanwhile in 1966 Rolls-Royce consolidated the British aircraft industry with the acquisition Bristol-Siddley Engines.

Suddenly in 1968, this company had something to do when it won a key order from Lockheed to build an engine for the TriStar aircraft. Although the contract seemed like a major step forward for Rolls-Royce, development of this powerful new engine, known as the RB211, took up far more time and money than Rolls-Royce had allowed for. This led in February 1971 to the company being on the brink of bankruptcy. It could only be saved by the British government, so Rolls-Royce was nationalised. There were debates about whether the car making division should be sold off. Instead, Rolls-Royce Motors at Crewe separated from Rolls-Royce Limited at Derby, but it was decided to merge the car company with British Leyland.

Rolls-Royce cars had always made money and this move was seen as a way of offsetting the huge Leyland losses. For a while it was business as usual, until October 1973 when the Arab-Israeli War broke out. The knock-on effect was reduced fuel supplies and a price that multiplied fourfold. To conserve fuel stocks, Prime Minister Edward Heath introduced a three-day week on 1st January, and there was a blanket national 50mph speed limit. The trade unions didn't like it which led to the miner's strike in

February 1974. Prime Minister Edward Heath called an election, which he lost. Now, Harold Wilson and the Labour government were now in charge.

Everyone went out and bought super-economical Minis, rather than Rolls-Royce Silver Shadows and the much smaller car became BLMC's best selling model. Unfortunately the minimal Mini profits were not going to help company finances, and throughout 1974 they desperately tried to find additional finance to keep going. BLMC didn't just talk to bankers – they also turned to the government. The Secretary of State for Industry, Tony Benn, who had so much to do with the creation of BLMC in the first place, made a statement to the House of Commons on December 6th. He said long-term there was likely to be some degree of public ownership. Obviously they weren't going to rush into this, although they did guarantee £50m of bank lending. Benn also made it clear that hand building cars for the few was going to end. Rolls-Royce became a subsidiary brand of Jaguar.

Almost immediately the Crewe factory was shut down and sold off. The Lord Mayor's, Funeral Director's and Wedding planner's favourite, the Daimler DS420 was the first model to be offered with the famous Rolls Royce grille. Jaguar XJs were now available with Rolls Royce badging and the Daimler Sovereign models discontinued. This was the branding mess that John Egan inherited when he was appointed as the boss of Jaguar. He approved production of the XJ's replacement the XJ40 in 1980 and in theory it should have been launched four years later. That was an ambitious target and he was determined to make it happen. Egan was very concerned about Rolls-Royce and knew that it was vital to go back to bespoke builds and a more distinctive model. For the time being Egan sanctioned a Rolls-Royce version of the XJ40 as part of a new beginning.

Egan certainly had to fix Jaguar first and raise quality standard by a huge degree. What he did though was very clever and allow teams of craftsmen to take the new XJ40 and then rebuild it and revise it to traditional Rolls-Royce standards. Re-engineering the model increased legroom, sound deadening and included fitting the Jaguar V12 engine. Although it was rumored to be an impossible job. However, with a team of specialist engineers dedicated to building customised cars, it was much easier. The V12 was also revised to make it more refined and significantly

quieter. This combination was a real winner and reignited demand for the model as Jaguar could charge a large premium. Rich people wanted them and that benefitted both Rolls Royce models, which became increasingly distinctive and helped to fund Jaguar with Egan at the helm.

Decades later Jaguar remains independent and successful with a range of luxury brands under its control with handmade Rolls-Royce at the top and a revived sporty mass produced Triumph as the well appointed entry level range. Somewhere in the middle are Jaguar saloons and sports cars. As for Bentleys, well those were the really quick ones and the Continental version of the XJS was a wonderfully characterful beast, but that's another story.

Autoreality: Jaguar Gets Owned

It was always about money with Jaguar, there was never enough of it. In July 1984, Jaguar was floated off as a separate company on the stock market. Sir John Egan is credited for Jaguar's unprecedented prosperity immediately after privatisation. In early 1986 Egan reported he had tackled the main problems that were holding Jaguar back from selling more cars: quality control, lagging delivery schedules and poor productivity. He laid off about one third of the company's employees. However, a favourable exchange rate in America and with all the development money spent on the new XJ, some argued it was difficult to fail.

Never mind Jaguar still needed money and Ford offered loads of their own to Jaguar's shareholders in November 1989. Jaguar never made a profit for Ford and as part of the Premier Automotive Group in 1999 they were lumped together with Aston Martin, Volvo and from 2000 Land Rover.

The X300 XJ was good, the S-Type and X-Type less so. Becoming glued to Land Rover for marketing and dealership purposes was helpful. When the two companies were being prepared for sale JCB were in line to buy Jaguar, but did not fancy taking on Land Rover as well, which would have been interesting. As we know the Tata Group picked up both brands. Meanwhile Rolls Royce is now owned by BMW.

You couldn't make that up.

23. The Routemaster Family

When it comes to British icons, specifically London ones, nothing says 'Good old Blighty' to the world more than a Routemaster bus. Introduced in 1958, the Routemaster saw continuous service in London until 2005. Despite retirement there are currently two heritage routes in central London. Obviously you can't put a good bus down and a brilliant one like the Routemaster is absolutely impossible to finish off. The thing is, not many people realise that there was not just the one Routemaster, it came in several different flavours.

There was the RM which was the standard bus and measured in at 27 and a half feet. Then there was the RML which was a rather longer bus that measured 30 feet. The RMC was a coach version the same length as the RM and didn't look that much like a coach, but it did have a proper electronically operated door rather than the open hop on, hop off rear opening that made it so famous and easy to use. Getting back to the RMC it was developed for the out of urban area Green Line routes. Indeed, they had modified suspension and interiors to allow a longer range and to be rather more comfortable. There was even an RCL version which was the same as the extended length as the RML, if that is not too confusing. Actually just to confuse the issue there was an RMF which had a front entrance, an RMA, a front entrance bus designated for British Airways which you used to see going up and down the M4 to Heathrow.

The thing about the Routemaster is that it was

purpose built, rather than being a lorry with a lot of seats as it was specifically designed by London Transport and then built by AEC. Indeed, the design brief was to produce a vehicle that was lighter, more spacious and easier to operate than before. The Routemaster was a groundbreaking design that used lightweight aluminum and techniques developed in aircraft production during World War II. As well as a novel weight-saving integral design, the Routemaster also introduced independent front suspension, power steering, an automatic gearbox and hydraulic braking. It could seat 64 passengers despite being almost a ton lighter than the old RT, that could seat a mere 56.

Routemaster production lasted just ten years when 2876 were built from 1958 to 1968. AEC though could see the bigger picture and wanted to develop the Routemaster into a range of commercial vehicles. London Transport were not interested in any further association, but would take a royalty on any spin off designs.

AEC believed that the agility and clever packaging of the Routemaster, especially the RMC version, could be adapted for use as a lorry for specific use in cities. Here was large commercial that was easy to drive and could fit into quite narrow streets. The side loading facility meant that it was easier where parking was restricted. Also, the security of the aluminum construction meant that it was harder to pinch anything from on board the AEC RCV. RCV stood for Routemaster Commercial Vehicle although most operators and drivers always referred to it as the 'Routemaster'.

Inside the RCV was not necessarily a double decker. It could be ordered with two storage floors, or even with seats at the top, or bottom. Most were supplied without the floor and had plenty of additional bracing to help the rigidity. Essentially It was a bus without windows and proved to be very popular all around the world. It was though expensive. A hand built lorry made to bespoke requirements was always going to be. However, the Routemaster name and the association with the iconic bus meant that companies regarded the RCV as a marketing and promotional tool.

AEC even downsized the Routemaster model by coming up with a van and a taxi version to rival both the FX4 and Ford Transit. The thing about icons is that they never go away. Despite legislation to clean the air over the

years and restrict commercial traffic AEC managed to keep up and meet demands from around the world for different powerplants and dimensions.

The most difficult period for AEC was the middle '70s when owners British Leyland dropped the AEC name in 1977 and then the factory in Southall Middlesex was shut in 1979. Routemaster production was suspended. It could have been the end, but following the example set by Jon Bloor buying and reviving the Triumph name, a consortium saved Routemaster in 1984.

As icons go, it is always pleasing to report that the Routemaster brand is still going strong and the badge proudly adorns a prestigious range of buses, lorries and taxis.

Autoreality: Routemaster Returns

On 3 September 2007, Conservative mayoral candidate a certain Boris Johnson announced that he was considering an updated Routemaster and scrapping the Bendy bus operation. That December Autocar magazine asked bus designer Capoco to come up with detailed proposals for a Routemaster.

Johnson backed the Capoco design in principle and suggested that he would hold a formal design competition to develop a new Routemaster if he became London mayor in 2008. After he was elected, this competition offered cash prizes for the winning entries. The results of the competition were published on 19 December 2008, with the winning and other good proposals being passed to bus manufacturers to draw up a final design.

Wrightbus in Northern Ireland were to build the bus Transport for London chose Heatherwick Studio to help design the bodywork. A full size mock-up was unveiled at the London Transport Museum's Acton Depot in November 2010.

Following Johnson's re-election as mayor in 2012, an order was placed for 600 and it was announced that they would all carry Northern Ireland registrations prefixed LTZ that matched the buses' fleet numbers.

There is masses amounts of detail about ventilation problems, batteries and other issues and so it was a complicated reimagining of what a 21st Century Routemaster should be.

24. Saab's very own Elk

Things were changing at Saab in the 1960s as the company realised that they had to build, bigger, better and more sophisticated cars. The two stroke engines were part of the problem. Endearing, and charcterful in a 96, but in a push to go profitably upmarket that smoky engine was a hindrance. The old V4 wasn't much better either. Saab tried to do sexy with the Sonnett, but it was strangely awkward coupe that never actually caught on. The Italian stylist Sergio Coggiola redesigned the Sonnett, but was hampered by Saab's insistence that he couldn't muck about with middle bit of the bodywork. The Sonnett soldiered on not being very sexy at all while Saab concentrated on developing the 99, which was going to get a four-stroke engine. That was an engine that Saab didn't have but Triumph certainly did.

Engineering and consultancy company Ricardo, had a general engine-development contract with Triumph, and was involved in developing a new engine for Saab. With a tight budget for the Swedes and knowing a new slant-4 was almost ready for production that brought Saab into contact with Triumph. That engine would end up inside the 99. The really exciting thing was that Ricardo knew all about Triumph's plans to join that engine together to make a V8. They mentioned that to the Swedes too and they were very interested. With their sights set on the highly lucrative United States car market, using a V8, an engine that American buyers understood and loved, made sense.

Initially Triumph were not keen on sharing their new big engine. So although the launch of the V8 engined

Stag was delayed until 1970 Saab never gave up pestering Triumph. Not only did they want the V8, but also the old six cylinder. Meanwhile problems were emerging with that engine. Overheating, timing chain failure, cylinder head warping and water pump failure among other issues. British Leyland were getting desperate so a token payment by a Swedish firm for an engine that didn't seem to work very well seemed like good business.

Saab increased the engine size of the four cylinder to 1.85 litres and in 1972 brought production to Scania for the 2.0 litre B version. That engine shared much with the original Triumph design, but was substantially redesigned. However, the V8 wasn't changed at all. All that happened was that Saab built it. Properly. Then installed it into a 99 to create the 99C V8. Then something incredible happened. America fell in love with the new model. Saab also went back to Triumph and bought the rights to the legendary six-cylinder unit and then set about making it even more efficient and powerful.

All of a sudden the plastic surgeons and dentists of the East and West Coast now had an alternative to the Mercedes SL in the shape of the 99C. There was a coupe and a convertible with a two-piece lift off hardtop. Unlike the Stag the convertible version of the 99C never needed structural reinforcement. It was also available with the six-cylinder and V8 engines. So as the Stag faltered in the States people started to call the 99C 'The Elk' as a nickname. It stuck and owners would even put their own chrome badges on the wings, almost mocking the British Stag. That was a bit of fun, but the serious business of making money meant that Saab became a rival for Mercedes and BMW both in Europe and America.

In the 1980s the Saab 99 remained as the smaller entry level model, the 900 was the mid size offering available as a saloon, hatchback and estate. An all-new 9000 was the big saloon and estate, which became a genuine alternative to the Mercedes S-Class. Even the Sonnet was reborn, this time completely restyled in Italy but still obviously a Saab. It was much larger, now mid-engined and when fitted with the V8 was something akin to a Scandinavian supercar.

Into the 1990s Saab was the first manufacturer to actually put into full production alternative fuel vehicles. Feedback from their research and development teams on the

AutoFutropolis – Car History Rebooted

West Coast of America had already seen them produce an entry-level roadster Sonnet to rival the Mazda MX5, also indicated that alternative power was a growing trend. Compressed Natural Gas and even injections of other natural products of the refining processes such as hydrogen were introduced. They also invested in biodiesel technology as an alternative to the alternatives. So without reengineering their products radically and concentrating on the infrastructure Saab managed to establish themselves as leading players in fuel supply. Saab and Scania Power Centres are now a familiar sight around the world. Not bad for company who took a risk on a V8 Elk.

Autoreality: Saab in the Open

Apparently Robert Sinclair who was the chairman of chairman of *Saab-Scania America*, reckoned there was room for a convertible. This was despite the cancellation of pure open top cars because of Federal roll over regulations.

With just $30,000 and a few months the prototype was unveiled at the 1983 Frankfurt Auto Show and was designated for production, which happened in late 1985. Meanwhile a proposal to produce a targa was rejected. So that's briefly how the 900 convertible actually came about and was finally built at the Valmet plant in Finland.

The Saab 9-3, was the last open topped model produced from 2003 until the company folded in 2011. There were no targas and after a brief flicker of Fisker involvement before Saab passed into the hands of the Chinese. Evergrande Group.

25. Nissan Scimitar Makes the Cut

It had all started so well for Reliant who had concluded that what world still needed was a small affordable and fun to drive convertible. With the demise of the Triumph Spitfire, TR7 and MGB and Midget the marketplace was clear for the little company to clean up.

So the launch of the Scimitar SS1 (Small Sports 1) at the NEC in 1984 signaled the beginning of a new era for Reliant. All they had to do was sell two thousand annually as per their projections and everything would be fine. Sadly things did not go according to that plan.

The reasons were two fold. First of all the car that every sporty driver wanted in Europe was a hot hatch. Things had moved on. The choice was either a British convertible that leaked or a continental built, quick, sharp handling and practical hatch. Oh and almost forgot there was a third very good reason why the SS1 did not prosper. It was ugly.

Even by the sometimes questionable styling standards of the 1980s the Scimitar was hard to look at for very long. What made it really sad is that the stylist was one of the true legends Giovanni Michelotti. Even sadder was that this proved to be his last job before he died.

Things were not going well and Reliant were already negotiating with Nissan about using their engines as a replacement for the Ford CVH. Meanwhile behind the scenes at the Japanese car company Nissan and the Government signed an agreement to build a car plant at the former Sunderland Airfield in February 1984. This wasn't as bonkers as building an ethical sports car in Northern Ireland, not least because the vehicle involved was an ultra reliable, properly engineered Nissan. Plus in the North East there were plenty of skilled manufacturing workers.

What occurred to Nissan is that they had an

opportunity to include an exciting British built sports car their into range. They planned to build Bluebirds from imported parts, but practicing on a smallish scale car to help develop car making skills seemed like a very good idea. This would not be a cheap option, but potentially it could be a vehicle with some global appeal. Being Japanese they loved the idea of a British sports car and had already heard very strong rumours that another rival company were spending time on the West Coast of America to develop ideas and concepts for something small and sporty. So it seemed only right that that the East Coast of England should give birth to something even more exciting.

Obviously the Scimitar handled sweetly and with a prototype Nissan Silvia Turbo engine on board, the performance was astounding. However, it looked atrocious and there was no way that Nissan would even think about having a plastic car in their range. Buying the Scimitar name and project was something of a relief for Reliant who could stick to making the Robin and commercial variants although even they could see that the market was shrinking. At least this cash injection would help.

Meanwhile Nissan set about styling and developing the Scimitar into something that they could be proud of. Rather than create a design that was brand new Nissan knew that taking inspiration from the past was the way forward. As much as they liked the idea of pop-up headlamps this was a complication that added, expense and weight, so out they went. As for inspiration it was suggested that they had taken a particularly close look at Healeys and come up with a rather more successful re-interpretation than the SS1.

So when Prime Minister Margaret Thatcher officially opened the new plant alongside Nissan president Yutaka Kume in September 1986, Bluebirds had in fact started to roll off the line back in July. The big and most surprising announcement of the day was the rebirth of the Scimitar, this time as a Nissan and not a Reliant.

The Nissan Scimitar was an instant hit. Just like the 1950s, production was very quickly focused on exports to the United States. The pent up demand was overwhelming and the majority of cars headed that way. Customers could choose between a basic 1.6, the fiery 1.6 Turbo with plans for a six cylinder and even a coupe' to follow on to make a range with a broader appeal.

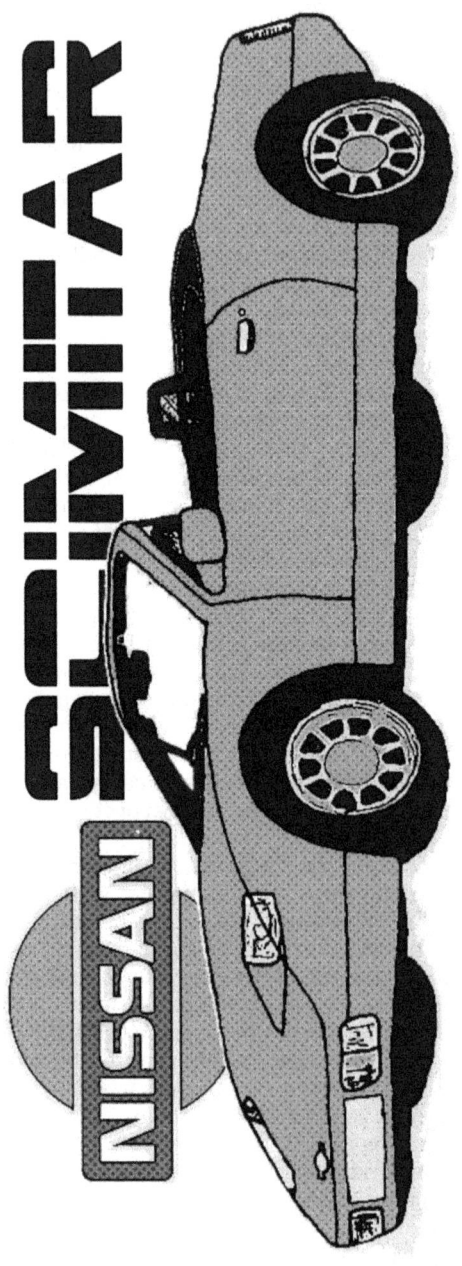

In California. Mazda quietly mothballed the roadster concept that they had been working on to rethink what they were going to do next. Whilst to this day the benchmark for so-called traditional sports cars remains the Nissan Scimitar.

Autoreality: Reliant Unreliable

Sadly the SS1 did not make it past 1990. A money losing, unpopular disaster of a model. However, the Reliant Motor Company was a busy place at the start of that decade. While they were making Robin's and Metrocabs the recievers started to pop in. Firstly on 25th October 1990. Bought by Beans Engineering for around £1.5 million it was then Beans turn to request the receiver assistance in November 1994. Reliant was then acquired by the Avonex Group in January 1995, who made it all the way to December before the receivers arrived.

From April 1996 a group led by Jonathan Heynes took the reins and by 1999 Reliant moved into import and distribution of the Ligier Microcar from France and the Piaggio Ape from Italy. Reliant introduced a new Reliant Robin Mk 3 Hatchback, but ceased making 3-wheelers in February 2001.

In April 2001 B&N Plastics announced that they would continue to make the Reliant Robin under licence. Unfortunately Reliant petered out by the end of 2002 when everyone had forgotten about the SS1

26. Sinclair's Electric Dreams Come True

Sir Clive Sinclair described his C5 "as revolutionary in its own terms as calculators in the early '70's or home computers in the early 1980's." And you know what, he was right.

The electric vehicle project started way back in 1973 when an in-house team of engineers began looking at ways of powering vehicles with electricity. More serious work started in 1981 at Sinclair Research, and in 1983 Sir Clive acquired the project personally from the company. A new company, Sinclair Vehicles Ltd, wholly owned and financed by Sir Clive was set up and moved to Warwick University's Science Park. Sinclair also consulted with Bert Hopwood the former motorcycle executive who took a close look at what was taking shape and wasn't at all pleased with what he saw. The proposed design was neither one thing (bike) nor the other (car). A tricycle was not a bad thing for stability, but the low stance made it difficult to see, the ride was awful and the plastic body looked cheap and nasty. Instead here was a chance to resurrect the Aerial 3, a unique scooter launched by BSA motorcycles in 1970. Although it had been a heroic failure as a two-stroke tricycle that tilted around corners, Hopwood knew where the tooling was and reckoned it could be reborn as a plug in electric bike that could revolutionise the 1980s.

Certainly replacing the noisy and smelly Dutch two-stroke with a simple electric motor and a battery, which was located in the box behind the rider, was a straightforward engineering solution. Ditching the pedals and installing running boards made it a solid platform. Buying the tooling was cheap enough and non-unionised labour with a Japanese attention to detail and quality in a purpose built Coventry factory certainly helped to make the tricycle as Sir Clive intended. The 1984 Sinclair C5 was promoted as a town centre shopping solution that made sense as pedestrianisation became the norm. For businesses and town dwellers it was the quiet and cheap way to get around. A contract with the Post Office certainly helped matters, as the red painted C5s became a regular sight on the streets with its big red parcel box on the back. It would last all day on a single charge winter or summer. This helped Sinclair's credibility as a manufacturer, but to be taken really seriously and make bigger profits they needed a vehicle, which could take a bigger payload.

It was a good job then that British Leyland had discontinued the Mini 95 Van in 1982. Sinclair moved swiftly and set about installing an electric motor under the bonnet and spreading the batteries along the load bay. This became the Sinclair C10 in 1985 and for the same reasons that the C5 caught on, the small van proved a big hit with businesses making local deliveries as the range was an impressive sixty miles and in stop start mode could easily last all day long with perhaps a top up whilst the driver had his lunch break.

Sinclair's electric delivery vehicles were going down extremely well with local councils who appreciated the reduced noise, and pollution. Sinclair suggested the creation of local hubs from which his vehicles could then take goods the final few miles. Donating brown field sites the authorities lapped this up as a way to free up the streets and generally look as though they had thought about this infrastructure initiative all along.

So as Sinclair effectively became a courier company, the profits increased and it was a short step to electrifying the Metro. Rover had seen how successful Sinclair had been with the C10, so co-operated fully to get the C15 as the electrified Metro van became known, made and then later a three door C20 hatchback and four door C25.

Sinclair had been very clever by never raising customer expectations too high too early. Meanwhile the battery technology was uprated, the range increased and making the batteries part of the chassis and design was the

next stage. Rover's ambitions were limited and they could not make the investment required to take electric vehicles to the next stage of development. That's when Sinclair started to work much more closely with the first Japanese manufacturer in Britain, Nissan. The lightweight Micra got the electric treatment first and soon the Electric Sunny as it was badged, became the first proper family EV.

So the two companies shared technology Sinclair badges stayed on the commercials as Nissan continued with the family friendly ones. As fuel prices fluctuated throughout the 1990s Sinclair offered stability for business and real value for the private buyer. Cleverly Sinclair had never got bogged down in the regulations and complications of actual car design. Instead they concentrated on the technology and that is why they remain the market leaders in electrically powered transportation solutions.

A good job then that Sinclair took a chance on an obsolete, outdated, out of production tricycle moped. Indeed, the latest heavily revised C5 remains the world's most popular EV as sales top 50 million.

Autoreality: Sir Clive Sinclair - Genius

Sir Clive Sinclair passed away on 16th September 2021. It time to reflect on his genius.

In the early 1970s he designed the pocket calculator so that it was affordable and not the size of typewriter. His first home computer, the ZX80 was named after the year it appeared. At £79.95 in kit form and £99.95 assembled, it was about one-fifth of the price of other home computers at the time and 50,000 were sold. It was followed by the ZX81, which cost £69.95 and sold 250,000. If you were a gamer or programmer this is where your career/enthusiasm started.

When it comes to transportation, his C5 was essentially an electrically assisted pedal cycle. However it was slower and less practical than a bike, with a range rated of around 20 miles from its 12V lead-acid battery, and a top speed of 15mph. It cost £399 and nobody was very interested. It wasn't Sinclair's fault, just a badly marketed product aimed at getting teenagers mobile rather than becoming the electrified answer to serious transportation questions. Incredibly he didn't give up and over the years continued to come up with some very credible alternatives to getting around.

The C5 itself derived from a prototype called C1, of which many running examples were produced in the late 1970s and early 1980s, which was intended to be the first of a series of electric vehicles.

Then there was the Sinclair Zike which weighed 11kg, and a small electric motor to drive the rear wheel, had its nickel-cadmium batteries - notable at the time for being half the weight of the equivalent lead-acid batteries - built into the frame and cost £499. There were three power levels to choose from, but just one gear, with assistance available for between 30 and 180 minutes, depending on how much electric shove you wanted. Top speed was limited below 15mph, in line with the law. The recharge time was one hour and the batteries rated as good for 2000 recharge cycles. Interestingly just 2000 were sold in 6 months, which was way below expectations.

Roll forward the Sinclair A-bike in 2006. It could fold into a bag, measuring just 67x30x16cm when collapsed and weighing 5.7kg. Wheel size was initially - and that's a crucial word, given it implies there were successors - 15cm in diameter, but later expanded to 20cm to boost stability.

Incredibly the A-bike spawned an electric variant in 2015, the electrical assistance was rated at 15 miles, the top speed 12.5mph and it measured 70x40x21cm and weighed 12kg.

Meanwhile, you might want to consider Sir Clive's nephew's Iris eTrike. It's still a Sinclair and if there is going to be any electric future it will be with small light two wheelers. Otherwise the Post Office were trialling out the future in the boxy shape of the Arrival van, well they were in 2017 anyway.

27. Siva Moon Buggy takes off...

On July 20, 1969, Commander Neil Armstrong became the first man on the moon. "That's one small step for a man, one giant leap for mankind."

Back on earth car designer Neville Trickett was inspired. If you were around in the late '60s the excitement surrounding the Apollo space programme was tangible. Everyone, whether or not they actually knew what a Saturn rocket was, fell in love with the romance and reality of space exploration. It suggested that the future was bright and out of this mundane world. That's why they bought Zoom and Orbit lollies, Kellogg's Sugar Smacks with a rocket on the front and Action Man got a space suit.

Neville Trickett was a very clever bloke and wondered how it might be possible to bring the Apollo mission back down to earth and onto the street. A good starting point would be the Lunar Roving Vehicle (LRV) which was a battery-powered four-wheeled vehicle used on the Moon during the last three missions of the Apollo programme, 15, 16 and 17, during 1971 and 1972. The LRV could carry one or two astronaut's equipment, and lunar samples. Trickett reckoned that all he needed to do was make sure that a two seat fun vehicle could cope with tarmac and ground clearance to handle a bit of loose gravel and mud.

Already in the late '60s their were artists impressions of what the moon car might look like and it was a sort of Beach Buggy. These were a phenomenon which was big in the USA and catching on in the UK. Trickett could see a way of bringing the two concepts together. Along with Mike Saunders who ran Siva this 'loony lunar' proposal would join the frankly bizarre model line up that included a Ford Popular based Edwardian roadster and Bentley Mk IV based specials.

The Siva Luna Rova was launched in 1971 just as the actual Lunar Rover hit the world's TV screens careering across the surface of the moon kicking up dust. Developed for rather less than the 38 million dollars that Boeing Aerospace and General Motors had spent, the British Rova was VW Beetle based. With the air cooled engine at the rear, knobbly tyres and sparse bodywork with mudguards over the wheels it looked enough like the one that was actually on the moon to catch on. Obviously that didn't stop NASA, Boeing and GM getting all worked up inside their space helmets.

A series of legal actions were begun in the States and the UK. Siva though didn't worry and just called the Luna Rova a Moon Buggy, which was perfect to chime in with the Beach Buggy craze. The American legal suits faltered, as the vehicle was never going to be sold there and in the UK the courts ruled in the company's favour. That was good, not least because the whole of Europe and Australia went Moon Buggy crazy. At least that offset the problems that the kit car industry suffered once VAT was imposed. The engine being over the rear wheels gave the light buggy a huge amount of traction so that it could cope with just about any terrain depending on the tyres. Here was a Caterham Seven for the adventurous generation.

Hardcore fans remade the old Luna Rover badges and added spacey touches (small TV aerial dishes) to their Moon Buggies. As the trend for building Beach Buggies faded away the Moon Buggy remained at the cutting edge with suspension and tyre developments which meant it never lost its off road edge. Customers could specify what they wanted and the bespoke element became the most profitable side of the Siva business. Apart from rescue vehicles there were racing series and all around the world, except the USA of course, the oddest of off roaders, a sportroader as it became widely known, thrived.

Then in the early 2000s a very interesting development occurred. Working on a hybrid electric system Siva managed to combine the weight of the batteries into the rear of the chassis and a much smaller air-cooled engine. So just like the original Lunar Rover it was now at least partly battery powered.

As the space programme wound down and NASA lightened up, Siva made an official application to register Luna Rova as a trademark worldwide. It was a small step for them, but a giant for humankind as finally every owner could finally say that had a genuine Luna Rova.

Autoreality: Man on the Moon?

The kit car business in the UK was very complicated, but let's look at. Neville Trickett's Siva Buggy. For £195 the kit included a fibreglass body and a steel tube chassis frame with most of the suspension headlights and rear lights, instruments, pedals and wheels from the mini. Inevitably the complete front subframe A-series engine could be bolted in. Bucket seats, a flat windscreen in an aluminium frame, 13 inch wheels and black vinyl hood were extras.

The moulds and production rights were sold to Euromotor in Amsterdam who had been the Siva-importer. They built cars offering them as the Siva Moonbug. Production ended in 1976 when a fire destroyed their premises.

Then again, did a couple of Americans actually land on the moon? There are a lot of theories out there, one bloke has been fairly consistent on this for over 20 years and Bart Sibrel's latest book is called Moon Man, but he has made a bunch of compelling films including, 'A Funny Thing Happened on the Way to the Moon', which you can catch up with online.

He believes the Moon landings were a hoax to hook the public's imagination and divert it from the Vietnam War. Sibrel cites the NASA aerospace engineer Wernher von Braun as another reason why the moon landings should be questioned. He said the Van Allen Belt – 272 miles from Earth – is impenetrable due to its high levels of radiation and a space rocket capable of reaching the Moon would need to be the size of the Empire State Building and weigh the same as the Queen Mary cruise liner.

Sibrel also claims the Moon is hit by mega micro meteorite storms every 48 hours capable of killing astronauts instantly and damaging space craft. "If it was so easy in 1969, there would be bases on the moon by now".

He might have a point, or maybe not, do your own research. The Siva Moonbug was very real.

Anyway, thank you to NASA for the below image of a prototype moon buggy being tested on planet earth.

28. Trab Trab Sputnik

Car building on the red side of the iron curtain was a confused affair in the immediate post war period comprising exiled German marques and factories with outdated equipment. A nationalised consortium called IFA brought together all the car plants in the East which built rehashed versions of the pre-war DKW Meisterklasse. However, an all-new car arrived in 1957 and was called Trabant, which translated means satellite. That's because the Soviets had just launched the first satellite in the round shape of the Sputnik. Indeed, Sputnik had caught the imagination in the West and the Communist Party saw an opportunity. However, the Trabbie was a nasty piece of work.

The Trabant had a steel chassis and frame that was made on huge presses which stamped out the basic shapes in a poisoness and deafening atmosphere. The bodywork was thought to be fibreglass, but it was hardly as sophisticated as that. Duroplast sounded good but the ingredients were shredded plastic, brown paper and cotton waste, all soaked in resin. Despite that it did look like a real car, but one that had been seriously shrunk in the wash.

Powered by a small 499cc engine, which grew five years later to a massive 594cc, but it could not operate as a four-cycle engine thanks to the Soviet restrictions. So just like a noisy, smelly, old two-stroke motorbike it ran on a combination of petrol and lubricating oil. Despite that the Trabant could reach a top speed of 62 mph and take all day to get there. It's specification was equally bad for all citizens. No one got a fuel gauge or an interior light. For most of its existence it made do with motorcycle type 6-volt electrics, although a decadent, capitalist automatic gearbox was eventually added to the otherwise non-existent options list.

Despite all these drawbacks the decision to rename the vehicle as a Sputnik for the Western market was a PR masterstroke. Not only that, the designers went to town in tacky 'outer-space' related cosmetic add ons. So the Duroplast body was sprayed a sort of spaceship silver and , decorative aerials were attached in random positions. It looked bizarre, but buyers in Western Europe lapped it up. Partly because it was a novelty. For some it did make a political statement, so trendy teachers would buy them. Others just liked the fact that it was a £200 car. It suddenly became an export only model from East Germany becoming a brilliant way to earn hard Western currency.

So the Sputnik carried on as an interesting curio in the car market until April 1966. That is when a Soviet Yak-28 jet bomber crashed into Lake Stößensee. The plane with a crew of two had taken off from Finow airport in the German Democratic Republic, but developed technical problems shortly after take-off. Captain Boris Kapustin and Lieutenant Yuri Yanov decided to land their stricken jet in the lake, avoiding the nearby residential areas, both dying upon impact.

That was tragic, but then the politics happened. The crash happened inside the British occupation zone, they were keen to take a close look at the wreckage, especially as the Yak-28 was often used as a spy-plane. It carried a sophisticated radar system known as the Skipspin which gave the Soviet fighter the capability to look up and down as well as ahead when doing scans. What the British army found next was completely unexpected. Hidden amongst the low technology embedded in the Duroplast was what turned out to be a tiny location beacon.

Apparently an invading Red Army would have been able to activate the beacons and then find the cars to help them advance further westwards, or even disable them to create roadblocks and get in NATO's way. It was a bizarre plan, but it meant that in many countries they were

confiscated and in some cases crushed. Overnight the Sputnik market collapsed and the dealer network throughout Europe was disbanded. The East Germans still had a captive market although that didn't make the waiting list any shorter. Lucky buyers still had to postpone their Trabant gratification for at least fifteen years. Yes, they quickly reverted back to the original name.

    Things carried on as before. The saloon was still called the Limousine, an estate version, The Universal, whilst there was even a military version (not one that just went beep like the Sputnik) which must have had some unspecified role. Maybe it involved poisoning NATO troops with a vehicle producing more than ten times the Hydrocarbons of a western vehicle from its exhaust pipe.

    Nothing showed the contrast between the two German peoples and just how their industries had fared over the last 28 years than the Wessis in their Volkswagen Golfs and Ossis in their Trabbies. A late engine transplant from a Wessi Polo failed to save it. The Trabant died in April 1991 and no one mourned. However, the values of surviving Sputniks continue to go through the Duroplast roof.

Autoreality: 34,500 still registered in Germany

Well, that was back in 2019, you never know that figure might nave gone up by now, although it is certainly well down on the post Berlin Wall fall figures when in 1993 about 900,000 were still registered in Germany.

It survived as a used car because of its low market value and modest, robust technology. However in 1991, the production was discontinued. Volkswagen settled in Zwickau, Chemnitz and Eisenach and developed the Golf and Polo models there. Opel has been producing cars there since 1992.

Mind you a new Trabant was launched at the Frankfurt motor show back in 2009. Obviously it would be an electric prototype produced German scale model manufacturer Herpa Miniaturmodelle GmbH. They wanted to get investors on board in order to finance a 2012 launch. That does not seem to have happened.

According to Herpa at the time, the new Trabant would have a rooftop solar panel for recharging its battery, a range of about about 156 miles and a kerb weight of less than 1000kg. IAV Automotive Engineering, based in Berlin, was building the electric powertrain. It didn't look half bad and better than the old two-stroke. Someone will probably try again.

29. Tucker The Swiss Carmarker

The first part of the Tucker story did not end well. Essentially the car company was broke. As a result they tried to recruit investors in highly creative ways. First, they sold dealer franchises and then they sold stock to the public. So even before a car had appeared they began to make car accessories like radios and seat covers, all to finance production of the Torpedo.

Trouble is the Justice Department and the Securities and Exchange Commission, did not regard this as very clever at all, just criminal and launched an investigation. They believed that Tucker was swindling the public and had no intention of building any cars. This was despite the fact that Preston Tucker and his workers managed to hand build thirty-seven cars to prove his point. A further fourteen were later built up from parts.

So the prosecutors struggled to convince the jury; in fact, the accusations were so weak that Tucker's lawyer did not even bother to mount a defence. Tucker was acquitted in January 1950, but the damage was already done: and he never built another Torpedo. Well not in America anyway.

Conspiracy theorists reckon that the established manufacturers in Detroit, Chrylser, General Motors and Ford were frankly terrified, firstly by the 300,000 advance orders and that an upstart car maker could offer such an advanced motor car. Indeed, this was just what attracted Tucker's new investors in Switzerland. They wanted to establish a strong European maker that combined quality and high technology. However, they were determined to keep a tight reign on expenses. The Swiss also wanted to make a fresh start. As impressive as the Torpedo certainly was it was the size was going to be a problem on European roads. Better to take all the brilliant elements of the Torpedo and include them in a fresh and more compact body.

A brand new plant was built in the Basel region with Tucker in charge and Torpedo designer Alex Tremulis as his right hand man. It was an ambitious project and it took four years to build the factory, design a car and get it onto the market in 1954. The Tucker Tornado, he loved alliteration, seemed expensive. Europe was still struggling to emerge economically from the financial strains of the Second World War, but prosperous Switzerland was ideally placed to embrace this home grown car. It also had the patience and deep enough pockets to wait for the nearby markets to mature.

The Tornado contained all the best elements of the Torpedo, except the engine was more conventionally relocated at the front of the car. However, there was nothing conventional about what was under the bonnet. Out went the helicopter related unit and in came a clever fully sealed Stirling cycle power plant which was smooth and powerful. Safety was priority with disc brakes all round and an enhanced hydraulic system all helped to stop the Tornado in half the distance of a contemporary rival. The entire passenger area was a safety cell, a development of the idea first incorporated in the Torpedo. Again, smooth surfaces, lots of padding and recessed controls meant that there was nothing to injure the occupants. Driver and passengers had a great view out as the wraparound glass area was maximised without compromise to the solidity of the structure. Aerodynamics was another feature carried over from the Torpedo, so that wind resistance was comfortably under their own 0.30cd benchmark. Meanwhile the doors were recessed into the roof so that getting in and out was never a problem.

The largely rubber suspension meant that it handled sweetly and rode impeccably, the perfect combination. Most importantly of all there had been enough time to properly develop the stillborn Tuckermatic transmission system. Here was a European car with standard automatic transmission, but it also had an optional clutchless manual override for those who wanted a sportier experience. Up front the third, centrally mounted headlamp that swiveled with the steering wheel would remain a feature of every subsequent Tucker.

The Torpedo was a remarkable achievement although Preston Tucker did not live long enough to see what an incredible impact it had on the car industry. He died at the end of 1956 of lung cancer, but the company lived on and prospered. The Tornado was joined by a much larger Torpedo and a smaller Tempest.

Always expensive, but exquisitely made with industry leading standards of safety. Tucker devised and adopted systems that included anti-skid suspension, foam roof passenger restraints and collision avoidance lasers. Safety conscious American couldn't get enough of the Tucker. Here was a Swiss car that became an export hit in the land of its very difficult birth.

Autoreality: Tucker the Truth

Preston Tucker had worked within Detroit for a long term and knew it inside out. His first job was an office boy for Cadillac before working on Ford Motor Companies' assembly line, all the time selling Studebaker cars on the side. In retailing full time he then went on to flog both Chrysler and Dodge. He joined forces with Harry Miller, with whom he would form Miller and Tucker, inc which created engines for the Indianapolis 500 and contact the Swiss-American Chevrolet Brothers who would later help him create the Tucker 48.

In the war years Tucker and his family moved back to Michigan where he began working on an armoured vehicle with the Tucker Turret a fast-traversing electrically powered gun turret widely described as having been mounted on aircraft and ground vehicles and small naval vessels.

After the war he built a car. A remarkable car. Only 51 Tucker 48's were ever built. Never mind the incredible safety features for the time, the car was also designed so the whole engine could be swapped with a temporary loan engine in just 30 minutes. He franchised over 1,000 dealerships to launch his new vehicle.

Take the time to seek out the 1988 film "Tucker, The Man and His Dream" not a half bad retelling of the story with Jeff Bridges in the lead role and directed by Francis Ford Coppola. In fact Coppola is himself a Tucker enthusiast and owns several.

30. When TVR went 4 x 4

The reality of TVR building a bespoke engine in the 1990s was always going to be problematical to say the least. Research and development at the major manufacturers always ran into the hundreds of millions and TVR only had small change. In many ways TVR's owner, Peter Wheeler was right to be thinking outside of the Rover V8 shaped block. When that engine came to its logical end then what on earth would the company do next? The simple answer is that they went to America.

There were good value V8s aplenty across the pond, but that wasn't the only reason for going as Wheeler and his team had ideas that would shock their loyal customers and win over a generation of new ones.

TVR was a typically British maker of sports cars, which meant that it was usually on the verge of bankruptcy. The cars were crude, brutish and established an enthusiastic following for their uncompromising behaviour. Between regular collapses, it was TVR dealer Arthur Lilley and his son Martin who brought calm and money to the company in 1965. However, it took another change of ownership to establish them as one of the most successful and uncompromising British sports car companies of the 1990s.

This happened when TVR owner and businessman Peter Wheeler took over in 1981. As well as pumping even more testosterone into the company's designs and engines he did something about the model names. Instead of Christian names he initiated a programme of calling the new cars after terrifying mythical beasts (although the first one was actually named after a Welsh postmaster... not really). So at the 1990 British Motor Show TVR unveiled a sensational prototype called the Griffith. It looked gorgeous and the public agreed as 350 firm orders were placed during the show. So for the rest of the 90s, the small company went on making cars with scary names (Chimera, Cerbera etc) and even scarier handling. It was a clever combination of massive engines and swoopy bodies with minimal safety devices.

By the late 1990s Wheeler was happy to change. He knew that to survive he had to sell cars to people who were not traditional TVR fans. So in the USA it was a good idea to combine a Ford 4 x 4 chassis and a V8 and they were happy to sell him the hardware. What he brought back to the UK was a new generation of TVRs that would not fall off the road so easily. Oh and they had power steering and ABS brakes underneath, with the unique plastic bodywork on top.

Wheeler broke it gently to the faithful. Firstly there was a Cerbera with four-wheel drive that almost anyone could drive. That annoyed the hardcore fans, but as they could still buy the rear wheel drive dangerous ones, they didn't really mind. The waiting list though for the new model got longer and it meant that TVR would have to relocate to a factory, which resembled something from the 20th Century. That required money, something TVR was earning in a big way now. There was talk of a link up with MG Rover as they scrambled about for an attention seeking sports car to take attention away from the fact that they didn't have any new models.

Wheeler managed to involve a complicated consortium of British based investors in 2000 and build new facilities. It was at this point that TVR threw that 360 degree turn and launched their 4 x 4. Yes really. The Arachna, that was Greek for spider, was an all terrain vehicle the like of which the world had never seen before. Like a spider it could stick to most surfaces and scuttle along at over 150mph.

In many ways it was a Cerebra on stilts and stretched a bit with added doors. The Arachna was insanely quick thanks to the Ford V8 although it looked very like the wrong car at the wrong time. However, what happened was that a lot of people finally understood this sort of tame and practical TVR and reckoned that this would be a super cool way of showing off while Range Rovers were still rather

lame and just as unreliable as TVRs. As traditional 4 x 4s became rather unpopular, TVRs continued to hit the spot for a select number of buyers who found them interesting.

Peter Wheeler passed away in 2009 but had set up a trust fund, which meant that the company would survive without him, but still with his maverick spirit. The winter of 2010, which was rather ferocious, meant that everyone wanted a 4 x 4 and the really rather interesting Cerbera 4 x 4 found an absolutely massive following. Many people thought why buy a Cayenne when a Cerbera 4 x 4 would be rather more fun and just a bit more interesting? The sales were largely in the UK but soon spread to Europe and the land of the ridiculous SUV, the US of A.

Meanwhile all that money meant TVR could carry on building the bonkers, dangerously beautiful sports cars and even think about making their own engine again.

Autoreality: TVR Rebirth Spiral

At the time of publishing this book fans of Blackpool's finest plastic sports cars were still waiting for something to happen. From the golden Wheeler age of the Chimaera, Griffith, Cerbera, T350, Typhon and Sagaris. Then in 2004 TVR swas old to Russian investor Nikolai Smolenski, but the company was struggling to justify its low quality products in an era when customers didn't just want short term thrills.

In June 2013, Smolensky sold all companies under

the TVR name to TVR Automotive Limited, lead by Les Edgar and John Chasey. The new company manufactured spare parts for cars on the road through the TVR Genuine Parts initiative.

Then in 2015 a new car was proposed and the intention was a 10-year plan to bring back road going TVRs starting in 2017. The car, codenamed T37, was planned to be a front-engined, rear-wheel-drive, Cosworth V8 powered car paired to a manual gearbox.

The new V8 engine would be based on Ford's Coyote 5-litre modified by Cosworth, featuring a lighter flywheel and dry-sump, unique engine management to make the engine produce loads of bhp.

In September 2017, the Griffith was unveiled to the public at the Goodwood Revival. Designed by Gordon Murray.

Ten months later TVR announced a £2m funding boost to help bring its Griffith to market, the marque has announced a new partnership with Ensorcia Metals Corporation. Though it hasn't disclosed how close this new backing brings it to its £25m funding target, it's said to help fund both production and development of the long-awaited Griffith and, duh, duh daah, a future electricity TVR.

Les Edgar, Chairman of TVR, said: "..it has been clear for some time that EV has to be part of our future. Finding the right partner for the road ahead has been a complex process."

A manufacturing facility was acquired by TVR in mid-2018, but, the Automotive Technology park in nearby Rhyd-y-Blew needed major investment to be readied for production.

The first Griffiths were due for delivery in early 2019, with a £40m in orders and secured funding from amongst others the Welsh government (which has a 3 per cent stake). However, TVR has pushed first deliveries to late 2023.

Then this happened, TVR's Chairman, Les Edgar stated: "Our collaboration with the ABB FIA Formula E World Championship and on-site activations at the Monaco and London E-Prix not only demonstrate our commitment to revolutionizing the TVR brand, but to EV, and becoming a sustainable, net-zero business. Our plans to bring TVR EV's to market are well underway, with the first of two models to be released shortly after the release of the newest Griffith and Limited-Edition Griffith EV models in 2024".

31. Vanden Plas in the USSR

There was only one thing on Harold Wilson's mind on January 23rd 1968 when he met Leonid Brezhnev and that was trade. The General Secretary of the CFSU Central Committee, wanted to talk about Vietnam and those nuclear weapons pointing in his direction in West Germany. Harold Wilson just wanted to sell cars. Hundreds of thousands of them.

Tony Benn the chairman of the Industrial Reorganisation Committee had told him before the BOAC VC10 departed that the newly formed British Leyland Motor Corporation was in deep trouble and they needed to do something radical. So exporting Austins and Morrises would be a jolly good start.

It was 20 degrees below freezing outside and although Brezhnev and Wilson got on well enough through the official translators, the British Prime Minister was surprised at just how animated the Russian Premier became when talk turned to cars. Apparently the Italians had beaten the Brits to it. They didn't need a people's car but Brezhnev did manage to grunt "Rolls Royce".

That wasn't as odd as it sounded, Vladimir Lenin had nine, including the world's only half-track Rolls, adapted with skis at the front for snow-driving. Wilson said he would see what he could do, to the utter consternation of his officials who didn't stop flapping until the VC10 landed back at Heathrow.

Luckily the Chairman and Managing Director of British Leyland, Donald Stokes was instrumental in culling a number of unprofitable models and among them was the underperforming Vanden Plas Princess. A strange old brew of a barge with loads of leather, wood and sound proofing, oh and a regal grille with a little crown, or rather coronet on the grille in black. These cars were built at BMC's Cowley factory and then sent to the Vanden Plas works at Kingsbury in London to get the posh bits bolted on.

Launched with a suitably big fanfare in 1964 and was so self-important that it had one of the longest model names in history. The Vanden Plas Princess 4-litre R Italic chrome script took up the entire length of the boot lid. The 'R' stood for Rolls-Royce, but that company had probably wisely decided not to take their version any further. Obviously much was made of the Rolls Royce connection, but the engine wasn't quite as whisper smooth and powerful as many expected.

Yes this outdated model was perfect for Russia agreed Benn and Wilson. The whole production line could go eastwards, and being communists they wouldn't want all those fancy parts that the Kingsbury plant threw its way.

MI5 were not at all happy about the Russians having access to an engine that was used in British military vehicles. If they were building a Rolls Royce engine they would just copy it. For that reason the Agency insisted that the 4.0 litre engine was replaced by the original BMC C-Series 3.0 litre. That didn't quite happen as planned. There was a bit of behind the scenes manoeuvring which saw two versions of the 4.0 engine being offered. This led directly to unsubstantiated rumours within the British Intelligence community that Harold Wilson was a KGB spy.

Meanwhile the Vanden Plas to Vladivostok deal went ahead. It was never going to be a straight cash deal, it involved quantities of furs, fish products (including caviar), manganese ore, bristles, flax and precious metals that came back in exchange. British Leyland then had to resell these in Europe and a separate company BL (Commodities) Europe was formed to do this.

Utilising an ex tractor parts facility, the location in the west of the Union meant that it was close to the borders of their allies in China and North Korea who could take delivery of the newest model from the Soviet Union.

Obviously they could not call it a Rolls Royce, but everyone knew what the Lenin RR was. It fitted just below the Zil and above the Volga and became very popular amongst the *nomenklatura*. They were the party officials

AutoFutropolis – Car History Rebooted

and key personnel in the government and other important sectors such as heavy industry. They loved the fact that it looked so much more modern than the dated Zils.

The Russians never did pare back to much on the leather and fancy wood as they had plenty of that, the Siberian Tiger fur roof lining was a bit much though. They did play down the chrome and fancy bits of trim that would collect dirt and rust on the exterior though. Recessed door handles also set it apart from the original model. Obviously the coronet was never going to stay on the grille, so it was replaced by a single red star. The most extreme model was the fabulous four-wheel drive Siberia, as it was badged in some export markets.

The Lenin RR remained available until the very early '90s when economic and ownership uncertainties saw it mothballed. However, The Russian Federation restarted production of the RR in 2010 having dropped the Lenin designation. The newly rich wanted a range of luxury vehicles and especially a 4 x 4 that they could call their own. And one of the biggest investors in this project? That would be the BL (Commodities) Europe, which continues to flourish as a huge conglomerate and trading company that was privatised in 1981.

Oh yes, out went the red star and back in came a golden coronet on top of the grille.

Autoreality: The People's Princess

First there was the Princess 3-litre in 1959 then BMC established the Vanden Plas name as a marque, and that led to the Vanden Plas Princess 3-Litre being created from 1960. The Vanden Plas 1100/1300 and 4-Litre R models which followed also bore the Princess name.

In 1974, the Vanden Plas Princess 1300 was replaced by the Allegro-based Vanden Plas 1500, so no longer a Princess. It was the last Vanden Plas and discontinued in 1980. Vanden Plas in Kingsbury itself made the Daimler DS420 limousine and tarted up the Double Six Vanden Plas as Jaguar Cars Limited were put in control.

Leyland Cars brought back the Princess name for the wedge 18-22 models. From 1982 to 1984 the Vanden Plas treatement was applied to the hatchback Ambassador.

British Leyland revived the Vanden Plas name on the 3500 Rover SD1, replacing the short-lived V8-S and a

2600 version was added in 1984.

Vanden Plas as a tarty trim level came back with a vengeance in the '80s with the badge being glued to the Austin Metro, Maestro and Montego. Incredibly the Honda based 213/216 range also got the same treatment and was the last VDP in 1989. Until that is the MG Rover Group produced a long wheelbase limousine version of the Rover 75 and let a coachbuilder add 200mm to the rear doors from 2002 to 2003.

Don't rule out VDP and Princess coming back into our motoring lives at some point.

32. Standard Go Off Road

Sir John Black, the Chairman of Standard cars had a predeliction for being towed around the factory grounds on skis at the first snowfall. That might sound a little far fetched but it was completely true and would eventually lead to the company reinventing itself.

In the post war climate of the late 1940s most car makers were not sticking to the one-model policy that the government was so keen to encourage. However, there were two exceptions. Rover's Land Rover and Standard's Vanguard. One was very good, the other very bad.

Standard already made the Ferguson tractor (there was a 12 year manufacturing agreement and they eventually used Standard engines) as proof that a simple, tough and practical vehicle was all you needed to survive after the war. At one point, the company was even building more tractors than cars. The Standard Vanguard, was bravely billed as "Made in Britain – designed for the World." An all-new model which in 1948 replaced the entire Standard range. Its body was attached to a separate chassis, which had all the important oily bits like the engine, gearbox and prop-shaft that took the power to the rear wheels. The gearbox was a three-speed job and it had something called synchromesh on the first gear, which meant that there were no more nasty grinding noises when drivers engaged that gear. There was a reasonably economical 2-litre engine, too, and it cost £544. Between 1948 and 1952, 185,000 found buyers. So it must have been brilliant then?

Even Sir John Black took part in the testing programme and was famously photographed in Wales putting the Vanguard through its paces, but that didn't help. Export models routinely broke down. The suspension, and indeed the whole structure of the Vanguard, was being shaken to bits. There were even cracks in the metal, which had occurred after just a few thousand miles.

Another car company seemed to have a better grasp on the one-model approach and that was Land Rover. Black was now paying very close attention and reckoned that he could learn a lot from what his rivals were doing. Having acquired Triumph, he had decided to make the most of the burgeoning sports car market in the United States, but Standard was rather more tricky. Although it was possible to sell bad cars when all new cars were scarce, he knew that product quality needed to improve as production ramped up in the 1950s. Not only that, a badly built saloon may not survive for long. Black reckoned that a more comfortable Land Rover would hit the retail spot.

So as the next generation Vanguard was being developed he turned to the man behind the tractors, Sir Harry Ferguson. Black negotiated a deal to use Ferguson's permanent four wheel drive system, utilising an open centre differential gear. Black also didn't think that buyers wanted anything too complex and specified an automatic gearbox as an option.

At the time though it was thought that the one major obstacle in the way of progress at Standard was the slightly eccentric Sir John Black. Some thought him increasing erratic, especially after surviving a serious car crash when he was a passenger in a prototype Triumph sports car. That didn't stop Black from declaring himself fit a week later and leaving hospital. At the works Christmas 'do' he did what every boss dreams of doing and said there were too many managers and named who should stay and go. The Standard board didn't like it one bit and on new year's day 1954 they turned up at his substantial house to sack him. After being announced by his butler, they presented him with a resignation letter to sign. He showed them an artists' impression of the Standard Shooting Brake, which was the future of the company. He was given twelve months

However, it took a while longer than that, but the

new Vanguard III from 1956 was a much better model. In particular the rather flash Sportsman which replaced the Triumph Renown. Even better the estate version was to be the basis for the Shooting Brake. It was an old fashioned name for a new type of vehicle, a high-rise, go anywhere set of wheels that was perfect for the posh country dweller, architect and those who aspired to be taken more seriously and climb the social ladder.

It didn't take long for the range to expand as Triumph versions which were introduced with 6 cylinder engines, roof rack and side step. Standard could abandon the ordinary Standards, run down production of the 10 and concentrate on making the highly profitable Shooting Brakes. Cleverly Standard offered a cheaper two-wheel drive example that proved just as popular. Meanwhile, Land Rover accelerated their Road Rover project.

Sir John Black was able to retire in triumph and spend his retirement driving to the Alps in his own Shooting Brake.

Autoreality: Standard Vanguard, not quite forever

Sir John Black believed that producing one model that could be built and used around the world was the best way to survive the 'export or die' post war car production climate. It wasn't called a 'world car' back then, arguably the VW Beetle was one mostly by accident and clever marketing, then there was Ford's world car, Mondeo and Focus to name just two.

The basic idea was excellent, the reality was that the early Standard in particular was not a well built, or comfortable car to own and a huge sales disappointment. Profits came from licence building Massey Ferguson tractors. There is a very complicated model history which is worth getting into, but overall the fortunes of the Standard marque faded while the more charismatic, sporty Triumph one was on the rise.

Triumph was to be the passenger car brand, but there were problems as the tractor production ended, Standard Triumph International was bought by Leyland Motors Ltd in December 1960. Although Leyland were committed to ending the Standard marque, production of a new Ensign de-luxe saloon and estate for May 1962 launch, was approved.

These became the last new British built Standard-badged cars, effectively Vanguard descendants with a 2138cc, 75 hp version of the original engine. The last British Vanguard models were built around a year later. The Standard survived through local production in India until 1988 when the last example of an unsuccessful Standard-badged Rover SD1 variant was built.

Meanwhile Standard's engines powered subsequent Triumph models, such as the Vitesse, the GT6 coupé and even the new 'Vanguard' which became the Triumph 2000 which stayed in production until 1977.

And finally, is a Shooting Brake really a four door estate? Aren't they always two door coachbuilt jobs? Anoraks might argue that, but I can tell you that drivers in the '50s and '60s called all estate cars Shooting Brakes.

33. Welcome to the Jet & Computer Age

Sir Frank Whittle had many reasons to feel let down by his country and he could have become a bitter and reclusive man. Instead, Whittle set about changing the way the world worked for a second time. When this engineering maverick joined forces with another genius who effectively invented modern computing, something epoch making was going to happen.

Whittle learned his engineering skills in his father's workshop as a lad before joining the RAF as an apprentice mechanic in 1923. He was promoted rapidly as his skills became recognised.

Sir Alan Turing did not enjoy his enforced stay at boarding school. Winning a scholarship to King's College, Cambridge was a turning point where he took a Mathematics degree. At just 22 he was elected to a Fellowship. At the same age Whittle invented the gas turbine jet. He sent his plans to the Air Ministry where the design was dismissed as "impracticable".

Meanwhile Turing published a paper that is now recognised as the foundation of computer science. He invented the idea of a 'Universal Machine' that could decode and perform any set of instructions. After two years at Princeton, developing ideas about secret ciphers, Turing returned to Britain and joined the government's code-breaking department.

Both men's brilliant ideas came to fruition in the Second World War. Whittle's revolutionary engine took to the skies for the first time, powering a Gloster E.28/39. Joined by other mathematicians at Bletchley Park, Turing developed a machine (the 'Bombe') capable of breaking Enigma messages.

Autofutropolis - Car History Rebooted

In 1946 Turing produced a detailed design for what was called the Automatic Computing Engine, a digital computer storing programs in its memory. His report emphasised the unlimited range of applications opened up by this technological revolution, and software developments. However, despite being a war hero bound by the Official Secrets, his private life was problematic to the authorities.

Post war Whittle's health suffered as his invention was given away to the American air force and most surprisingly, the Russians. So he retired from the Air Force in 1948. Whittle decided that there was freedom and backing to develop his ideas in America. He was one of the few to know just how crucial and important Turing's work had been so asked if he felt like relocating to the warmth and relative freedom of California. The Whittle & Turing Corporation was formed to make the world a better place.

Whittle had for some time seen the gas turbine's potential to power road vehicles, being simpler and more powerful than an internal combustion engine. Whittle & Turing Corporation of California would not make vehicles but would design and patent all the systems. Manufacturers would come to them.

There was already a connection with Rover cars that had been commissioned to build and even develop jet propulsion to the extent they were already experimenting with their JET 1 prototype. Whittle believed he could do it better and anyway did not want to work in the UK, or with a British based companies again.

A gas turbine engine has a number of things going for it. It is inherently very clean, and can run on just about anything as the high combustion temperature means everything burns. That included petrol, paraffin, and diesel although Whittle had a preference for Liquid Petroleum Gas. The unit is also very compact and lightweight. Simply adding waste gates before the power turbine meant there was no need for a clutch, so it operated like a constantly variable transmission, but without the complication of any gears. Maintenance was always minimal.

Using water injection boosted the miles per gallon and reducing the revolutions down below 20,000 seemed a tall order, but Turing's control systems changed the behaviour and improved the fuel economy even further. Instead of struggling to get more than 10mpg that the Rover managed, their unit could return well over 30mpg, on the

AutoFutropolis – Car History Rebooted

test bench anyway.

Chrysler and General Motors were already developing their own systems, but the Whittle & Turing Jet engine was production ready and seemed to work in the real world. That probably explains why Ford was so keen to jump ahead of their rivals and install it initially in the charismatic Thunderbird and call it the Thunder Jet.

Meanwhile Turing was keen to add new systems to vehicles such as a much improved cruise control systems and also automatic guidance. This led directly to the Universal City. Here was the grid system layout taken to its logical conclusion. Turing proved that it was possible to control and regulate the traffic system with an Automatic Computing Engine, which was more powerful and effective than anything that IBM could offer at the time. Universal City Ready vehicles were self-driving and the owners could input their zip code destination. Early adopters included Los Angeles who recognised that pollution and congestion were two serious issues that technology could help solve.

So the combination of Whittle's fuel efficient and clean turbine engines and Turing's integrated Universal Cities changed how vehicles were powered and managed globally. Their company was a force for good as it delivered new inventions, concepts and products from their offices in the so-called, Jet Car Valley.

Autoreality: Chips and Jets with everything

Manufacturers began introducing early versions of computer controlled systems to perform one specific function. In 1968 Volkswagen introduced a computer controlled electronic fuel injection (EFI) system - the D-Jetronic, a transistorized electronic module from Bosch on their Type-3.

There is a long timeline of electric control units being installed into cars making them better and more complicated over the years. For example in 1973 all American Chrysler models came with an Electronic Engine Control and in 1978 - Mercedes-Benz in partnetship with Bosch introduced the world's first anti-lock brake system (ABS).

When it comes to Jet propelled cars, that never really caught on, but they did exist when in 1950 Rover built the first gas-turbine powered car: Jet One with a T8 gas turbine fitted to a P4. Development continued over the years. In 1963 The Rover-B.R.M. Gas Turbine Car was the first to complete the Le Mans 24 hour race but not as a contestant. Then in 1965 a regenerative heat exchanger was fitted it was the first British car to cross the finish line at Le Mans. After that it gets dreary as Leyland become involved the turbines built for various commercial applications. Turbine lorries could have been a thing, but they didn't happen either.

In America it was more exciting. Chrysler made their road going turbine car in 1963 as a two-door hardtop. The exterior and interior color was called Turbine Bronze. These Chrysler Turbine cars were built at a rate of one per week until the last of the 50 cars were finished in October 1964. Their Turbine program tested consumer and market reaction to turbine power and get service data and driver experience by giving them to real members of the public. Much was made at the time when Lynn A. Townsend, president of Chrysler Corporation at the time, presented the keys of the Turbine car to Mr. and Mrs. Richard E. Viaha of Broadview, a suburb of Chicago.

Clearly it didn't go well enough and the costs involved were too high. Quite a clever PR stunt though.

34. Vauxhall Vulcan Out of this World...

General Motors designer Wayne Cherry was given the opportunity to create a concept car for Vauxhall as a way to annouunce that the company had a new Luton based Design Centre. Cherry joined GM in 1962 after graduating from the Art Center College in LA, and moved to Luton in 1965. He came with a coupe called the XVR which stood for eXperimental Vauxhall Research. Three examples were built and shown at Motor Shows and other venues around the world in 1966. It looked like a Chevrolet Corvette and it was a shame it never lived to be sold next to Vivas and Victors in a Vauxhall showroom.

As assistant design director Cherry carried over some of the design cues into Vauxhall production cars. He was commissioned along with his team that included his colleagues Chris Field and John Taylor to come up with a Styling Research Vehicle (SRV). It was slated to be shown at the 1970 London Motor Show. General Motors liked what they saw with the initial sketches and were prepared to finance some full scale working prototypes. Rather than reveal all with a concept they decided to build a four door, four seat sports car that looked like a Le Mans racer.

Indeed, what General Motors intended was to upend the whole staid saloon car market with something quite radical. It had a long tail and a cabin forward seating position within the huge of the 5.08-meter-long bodywork. Cherry proposed mobile aerodynamic aids for the SRV via a pedal in the cockpit that could adjust an aerofoil in the nose section. At the same time, an electrically operated levelling system was provided for the rear axle. This was a complication that General Motors didn't need. Also the instruments that moved outwards with the drivers door on the proposal and early prototypes was interesting but a bit much. Engineering the big doors would take plenty of man hours and resources.

Crucial to the design was a rear engine layout and the overall ease of changing the power unit, but which ones? The radical aerodynamics and low height meant that a V8 was not entirely necessary. This seemed like a wonderful opportunity to use General Motors extensive research and development when it came to turbine propulsion. Potentially this allowed lots of different fuels to be used. Not only that a conventional V6 would be the basic powerplant as it was felt that the styling could frighten away buyers.

Actually the whole SRV concept was in search of a brand badge and General Motors had plenty of those to choose from. Certainly the SRV might be too radical for the upmarket Cadillac, or staid Oldsmobile. However it could thrive as a Pontiac and certainly make sense as a performance focused Chevrolet Impala V. What about Vauxhall though who were designing the thing? Effectively it would be a replacement for the huge breeze block shaped Cresta, but would there be takers for something so large and different from the norm?

Decisions were taken and yes it would be a European model too, the Vauxhall Vulcan in Britain and the Opel Commander on the continent. They would have conventional four cylinder 2.3 and 3.0 V6 petrol engines. In the rest of the world, but mainly America a Chevrolet with a V6 engine and the turbine Pontiac GTV. Actually the turbine was an inspired option because while all car sales suffered in 1973 with the fuel crisis, the GTO+ boomed. The car buying public lapped up the wedge shape in the world's largest marketplace. It was futuristic and with Chevrolet's value for money pricing this was the family saloon car of choice. Indeed, a super luxury version with a Cadillac badge was almost inevitable. Over in Europe the Vulcan and Commander were the prestige big saloons that were trouncing the Jaguar XJ and was now a strong rival to the Mercedes W116.

One interesting diversion was into motorsport. It may have seemed a bit late in the day, but the vehicle which looked as though it actually belonged on the race track, went there and won. Targetting the endurance events such as the Nuburgring 24 hours this ambitious programme culminated in back to back Le Mans victories in 1975 and '76.

These V series Vauxhalls never actually went away. Although they have been updated in line with safety and environmental legislation over the years, the shape stayed current despite a tricky late '80s period when they could have been retired. At the top of end, luxury and prestiege buyers still loved the looks. The engines varied around the world from common rail diesel era, there was even enough room for a Hybrid drivetrain batteries respositioned at the front end and in the sills. Finally the V series was perfect as an early adopter of Electric propulsion.

Incredibly it still looks and drives like the future.

Autoreality: SRV – Still the future in 1977

It was always a concept and never hit reality and the chance to make a spectacular impact.

Purely a styling exercise and not a functional vehicle it was supposed to be powered by a transversely mounted dual overhead cam (DOHC) 2.3-liter slant four engine with fuel injection and twin turbochargers. The interior had fixed front seats with adjustable driver controls, steering column, and pedals. The instruments were fixed to a pod hinged to the driver's door. There was an electrically adjusted suspension leveling at the rear, and rather cleverly the fuel could be re-distributed to different tanks to adjust handling.

It sort of worked, although the engine dummy was made from glassfibre wood and metal. But there was a proper monocoque rolling chassis, with the fixed front seat bases both pedals and steering column were movable – forming part of the structure. Tubular subframes carried a beam front axle.

The SRV first appeared at the Earls Court Motor Show in October 1970, it was put on display at the Geneva Motor Show several months later, in 1971. It was still being shown as 'a glimpse into the future' at the Scottish Motor

Show in October 1977 and was touted as 'a look ahead to the possible Vauxhalls of tomorrow'. That's how far ahead the design still looked.

Retirement eventually beckoned and it lives out its stationary days in Vauxhall's Heritage Centre.

Here it is outside the Heritage Centre and thanks again to Vauxhall for some wonderful behind the scenes pictures of how it came to together and was displayed at Motor Shows, plus a contemporary spec sheet.

Wayne Cherry

Styling Research Vehicle by Vauxhall

The S.R.V. – Styling Research Vehicle – is a three-dimensional exercise by Vauxhall's Styling Department to suggest the form in which various specialised design and layout problems may be solved in the future.

A high-speed, 4-door, 4-seater only 41½ inches high, it is envisaged by the stylists to be powered by a transverse engine, boosted by turbo-charger and mounted midships behind the passenger compartment.

All four passengers and the engine are accommodated within the wheelbase. The front seats are fixed, but control pedals, steering column and front-seat rake are adjustable to suit individual driver's requirements. By locating the front seats in a fixed position, the seat structure can be designed to contribute to the overall strength of the car's frame which completely surrounds the passenger compartment.

All control switches are mounted in the driver's door and are grouped in sequence, as in an aircraft cockpit. The instrument panel is mounted to the side of the driver and swings outward as the door opens to facilitate entry and exit.

The S.R.V.'s design also incorporates a number of novel proposals for aerodynamic research at high speeds. Such as ideas for 'trimming' the car in motion by the use of an aerofoil in the nose, an electric levelling system at the rear, and – following aircraft practice – a pump system to re-distribute fuel load among a series of storage tanks.

Instruments shown on the panel mock-up on this model relate, apart from speedometer and tachometer, to the research equipment envisaged as being installed in the vehicle. They include manometer designed to collate air pressure readings from measuring points over the surface of the car; a fuel distribution gauge; three instruments relating to the turbo-charger – boost gauge, tachometer, and exhaust-gas temperature gauge; and digital clock to maintain a time-scale on an automatic data recording unit. Additional instrumentation is also provided on the sill inside the trunk at the rear.

Dimensions

Length	16 ft. 8 in.	(5·08 m.)
Width	6 ft. 4½ in.	(1·94 m.)
Height	3 ft. 5½ in.	(1·05 m.)
Wheelbase	8 ft. 9 in.	(2·67 m.)
Front track	5 ft. 2¼ in.	(1·59 m.)
Rear track	4 ft. 4¼ in.	(1·32 m.)
Front overhang	3 ft. 7½ in.	(1·10 m.)
Rear overhang	4 ft. 3½ in.	(1·31 m.)

VAUXHALL MOTORS LTD. Luton Beds

And that was where I was going to leave it. The thing is though, car manufacturers do come up with some fabulous creations for the purposes of promotion and just throwing mad ideas out there. The great thing about the Vauxhall SRV is that I didn't have to do a silly drawing for it , that there is a wonderful back story better than anything I could ever make up.

So here's a tacked on but very interesting Chapter for your reading pleasure about all the other manufacturers who decided to produce something a little different as a one off for a motor show or a genuine blue sky proposal...

35. Conceptualism - when manufacturers thought out of the boring old saloon/hatch/estate/pick-up box...

Once upon a time there were events called motor shows. Hopefully they will make a return, but these wonderful gatherings existed so that car manufacturers could show off.

Not just their latest dreary family shifting profit making fodder, but proper, mad as a lorry, flights of fancy. These were often weird cars that looked good on the display stands and showed other manufacturers that they were planning ahead for something or other.

For customers of their regular wheels it was a dream that one day they might be able to part exchange their way into one. Significantly concepts cars don't have to work. They could be made out of cardboard and sticky tape so that from a distance they looked sexy. They just wouldn't take you to the shops or do the predicted 250mph. But that was OK, this is fantasy car building to impress the industry, give gullible journalists something to write about and look good in the magazines.

The Mercedes C111 went on making an impact for many years after it was built, similiarly the Vauxhall SRV never went out of fashion and Jaguar XJ13 is a real 'what could have been'. It is always great see that big companies were thinking so far outside of the car design box, that it is probably octagonal. Or at least pyramid shaped like the Citroen Karin. Indeed, when the concepts are done properly they are very much what AutoFutroplis is all about.

So here is a random selection of interesting concepts. I think a lot of the American 1950s ones are properly space age, but otherwise everything from the '70s and '80s that is wedge shaped with pop up headlamps and a lady standing next to it, is of course truly wonderful. We have some of those to consider, plus a whole bunch of other vehicles which rarely became anything else. There are exceptions of course and the Audi TT for instance stayed remarkably intact from dream to reality once plonked on top of a Golf, so it can be done.

Ferrari 512s Modulo 1970 This is what Ferrari should have done a lot more often. Pininfarina did the styling and what a wonderfully wedgetastic thing it is. It was black at the Geneva Motorshow and later repainted white, which shows off the lines a lot better. It won 22 awards, so designers must have thought it was good. Power came from the V12 engine that delivered 550hp and potentially a top speed of 220mph. The only person who can find that out is American film producer James Glickenhaus who in 2014 bought the car from Pininfarina with the intention of restoring it to full working order.

ItalDesign Machimoto 1986 Italian for "car" and "motorcycle," delivers Machimoto and that is pretty much what ItalDesign delivered. Just in case you wondered, every one of the six seats was a motorcycle saddle. It was designed to take up to nine bodies and to be an economy model. Essentially it is a funky people carrier. Imagine taking the family out for a spin in this, ideally wearing helmets. Incredibly it was based on a Volkswagen Golf with a 1.8 petrol engine. It would have been slow with nine on board.

Lancia Medusa 1980 If only Lancia had made this they may not be in the terminal decline which could lead to possible extinction. This is a reimaging of the family car which would have made a contemporary Mercedes 200 and BMW 5 Series look rather dull and boring. It was designed to be spacious and practical. Never mind that it had a mid-mounted engine which might have comprised some of the packaging, but at least they were doing something different. The pop-up headlamps were very welcome and give it bonus points. The Medusa, which maybe you should not look at, also had a funky interior with a button fest on the steering wheel. You can never have enough buttons.

Toyota CX-80 1979 If you pitched up to the Tokyo Motor Show in '79 you would have seen this hard to miss 'car of the future' which was fuel efficient, light and compact. It was front-wheel drive and inside it was all rather Atari and a steering wheel with buttons. They should have stuck a Starlet badge on it and put it in the showroom.

Autobianchi A112 Runabout 1969 Apparently inspired by speedboats of the era which did without windscreen wipers, most of the windscreen and doors. The speedometer actually looked like a compass. Marcello Gandini working at Bertone came up with shape which pretty much came back, with doors, a windscreen and a targa top as the Fiat X1/9. A concept that deservedly became real.

BMW Turbo 1972 This is the first time BMW did a concept and what an absolute corker. Internally known as the E25 Turbo, it was built to celebrate the 1972 Olympics. Paul Bracq did the design and it was built by Micholetti in Turun. This gull-winged beauty's turbo engine would get it to 60mph in 6.6 seconds. Just two were built and it effectively came back in the shape of the magnificent M1 in 1978.

Alfa Romeo Navajo 1976 Here was a Bertone designed car based on Alfa's race car chassis and the 33 Stradale. It was light and compact and powered by a 2.0-litre V8 engine producing 230hp. Bertone built one and the asking price would have been £3m at the time. It was one of six one offs from all the best known designers based on the 33 and this was probably the pick of that collection.

Ferrari Pinin 1980 This Ferrari came about as a celebration of Italian design studio Pininifarina's 50th-anniversary celebrations. What a handsome thing even if it does resemble a Vauxhall Senator complete with egg crate grille. It was built on the lengthened chassis of a Ferrari 400GT with a dummy 512BB engine. The car was mocked-up with a 4.8-litre flat V12 engine but didn't actually run until 2010 when an engineering team was given the task of getting the vehicle working when it was bought by Jack Swaters the Belgian importer. Mauro Forghieri was the famous engineer who made it happen. It is a shame that it never became a production car, but Enzo Ferrari was very much alive at the time and not surprisingly protective of the sports car brand. It is not as if the company would ever build a four door vehicle is it? Oh what's this the Ferrari Purosangue? Not a great name.

Citroen Karin 1980 This what you want Citroen to do, something genuinely bonkers and here it is. It had a centre mounted steering wheel and a three-abreast seating configuration. Unveiled at the Paris Motor Show, it was created by Trevor Fiore, who was responsible for the Citroën design centre at the time. The driver's seat was central and positioned slightly ahead of the two passengers, many years before the McLaren F1.

Renault Fiftie 1996 To mark the 50th anniversary of the 4CV at the 1946 Paris Motor Show, the company decided to indulge in a bit of retro reinterpretation. It was thoroughly modern with a carbonfibre body mounted on the aluminium frame of the Renault Spider sports car. Its new, rear-mounted D Engine was subsequently fitted to the first-generation Twingo. Considering how well the revived Beetle and MINI did, maybe Renault should have taken the Fiftie further.

Ford Fiesta Fantasy 1978 And what a fantastical little thing this was. Pick ups come in all shapes and sizes and this is pocket sized and not just a pick up. Built to celebrate Ford's 75th birthday and shown at the Chicago Auto Show it was a clever package. Glassfibre body panels allowed the Fantasy to also morph into a, a four-seater convertible or a two-seater coupé. Wonderful.

Volvo Tundra 1979 Here is another design classic from

Marcello Gandini working for Bertone. It seems that Volvo wanted the 343, to be less dreary, but this was rather challenging, although it might have inspired them to create the 480 a few years later. Anyway, Citroen were always up for doing something different, not Karin different, but the French took the Tundra and Gandini turned it into the BX.

AMC AM Van 1978 Underfunded American Motors at least had some flair and imagination. They showed what they could do on their Concept 80 Tour in 1977. This van was one of seven vehicles which took in seven cities. This was the stand out, a two door van equipped with 4WD. It was promoted as a "Go-anywhere four-wheel-drive vehicle with excellent potential for recreational and utility use in addition to family transportation." Unfortunately it was a dummy vehicle, so it just looked good without going anywhere at all. It is interesting that AMC saw 4 x 4 as the future when a few years later they launched the Hornet and Eagle with extra ride height and all terrain ability. For the time being buyers had to make do with the Pacer Wagon, a two door cube of an estate.

Pontiac Trans Am Type K 1977 K stood for Kammback, basically a breadvan style that made it more practical and also aerodynamic. It went down well as a concept and it was actually considered for production involving Pininfarina who supplied the unique rear body panels. It would have been pricey though. Two were made and one with a Trans-Am front end got a bit part in the Rockford Files TV Show.

Fiat 126 Cavaletta 1976 Here is cute reinterpretation of the 126, a vehicle which was around for 26 years

unchanged. This would have been interesting as a recreational almost Mini Moke like, but with a decent roof rather than a leaky canvas job.

Nissan Cypact 1999 This weird looking tiddler could have out KA'd the Ford KA. The 1.2-litre turbodiesel delivered a claimed fuel economy figure of 83mpg. Interestingly it had an Intelligent Transport System, early Sat Nav which let you know of any problems getting to the preferred destination.

Ford 021C 1999 talking of Ford Kas this was pretty much the same size, being shorter, but wider and taller. It certainly looked very designery which was no surpise as industrial designer rather than car stylist Marc Newson did it and Ghia built it. Made it to the London Design Museum. Powered by a 1.6-litre petrol engine driving the front wheels through an automatic gearbox.

Jeep Jeepster 1998 Although Marc Bolan said he was a Jeepster for your love, the name has been around since 1948. According to Jeep this was designed to be capable of crossing the 22-mile Rubicon Trail in the Sierra Nevada mountain range, hence the Jeep models with that name. The ground clearance was adjustable over a range of four inches. Looks fairly mean and had a 4.7-litre V8.

Jaguar XK180 1998 This arrived at the 1998 Paris Motor

Show, 50 years to the month after Jaguar's first XK, the 120, made its debut at Earls Court. Based on a shortened, rebodied Jaguar XKR with its supercharged 4.0-litre V8. It proved that Jaguar could still make head turners, if they wanted to.

Nissan Stylish 6 1997 Shows us that a big car company still had faith in the estate car format. It had six seats arranged in two rows of three and a six cylinder 2.5 petrol-electric hybrid powertrain, and used a CVT transmission. Great model name.

Briggs and Stratton 1980 Yes the people who made your mower engine, once did a car. A fabulous six wheeled car that had its finger on the future zeitgeist of alternative propulsion. Here was a hybrid before anyone knew what that meant. First off there was a 18-horsepower air-cooled twin-cylinder Briggs engine, pretty much a couple of push mower engines joined together. Not only that, an electric motor is connected to the engine, which is in turn attached to a four-speed manual transmission sending power to the first set of rear wheels. Technically this was a parallel hybrid, meaning it can run solely on the petrol mower engine, the electric motor, or a combination of both. Six 12-volt batteries were installed and when fully charged the Briggs and Stratton had an estimated electric-only range of around 50 miles. Which should get you to a petrol station for a top up.

Just in case you wondered the car itself wasn't made from sundry mower parts, so the front suspension, steering, and transmission come from a Ford Pinto. Then it was over to Volkswagen and their Scirocco for the doors, dashboard and windscreen. Everything else is Briggs and Stratton.It was supposed to work like this, the electric motor and its instant torque would get the car up to speed, at which point the petrol engine could be used to provide the momentum. You can just wonder at the majesty and ambition of a small engine maker thinking ahead of every major car company on the planet. I now want to create a scenario where Flymo come up with a rather interesting vehicle which does not touch the ground. Or even the grass. It manages to seemlessly travel to its destination as if riding on a magic, motorised carpet. And there was me thinking that AutoFutropolis 2 would be a really stupid idea.

37. That time I 'drove' a Concept that became Reality –

I would like to take the credit for this Isuzu going into production four years later, but actually all I did was hang around with the makers as they made a promotional film. I was despatched by Car Magazine when Mark Gilles was briefly in charge to write a proper journalistic scoop type feature.

It was late September 1993 and I flew from Stanstead to Glasgow with photographer Colin Curwood. There we hired a Ford Fiesta and drove north. We stayed in a quaint Hotel near Fort William which was packed full of American tourists and us and Isuzu. The next day we were on set, which was essentially the Highlands. They were shooting a promotional video which would run at the Japanese Motor Show in just over a month's time. Designer Simon Fox was driving and there was a pretty photogenic model as his passenger.

Colin was not happy as he had to work around a film crew and I had to wait for lulls so I could talk to the important people. However, I have a confession to make. I didn't drive the Vehi-CROSS. No way I could really. Too risky for Isuzu. The vehicle was priceless and it had to get on a plane and fly to Japan. So they rightly said no. I sat in the passenger seat in the dark for a final run when it was too dark to film. Driving it though was the story so that lie had to stay in, so please don't believe anything you read in magazines, newspapers, or watch on television. Here are my original notes reproduced for the first time and a couple of snaps I took on the day that have never been seen before...

Isuzu Vehi-CROSS Driving the to the Future in saloon car comfort, but ready to off road at any moment...

Officially, it does not exist, yet I'm sitting in the driving seat. The instruments are illuminated mock-ups, but the controls, engine and drivetrain are the real thing. It's getting dark and there is just time to negotiate a single track road deep in the Scottish Highlands. If for any reason this priceless vehicle does some premature crumple zone tests, Mr. Isuzu and the business end of a Samurai sword would probably want to know all the details. It's frightening, it's exhilarating, it looks like nothing that's ever been driven on this planet before; it is an Isuzu Vehi-CROSS.

I've just spent the day with an off-roader that could change the way you think about Isuzu in general and 4 x 4s in particular. Before highlighting what makes the Vehi-CROSS concept unique when compared to any existing dual purpose vehicle, it is immediately obvious that this is a show car with a difference: it actually works. Whilst most manufacturers and design studios are happy to mock-up a car that looks outrageous in practice and goes like the clappers in far fetched principle, the Vehi-CROSS manages to do both, in real life. Although destined for static display at the Tokyo Motor Show, Isuzu are kind enough to let it go on an outing with us to the wilds of Western Scotland, on one condition: that they get it back in one piece.

So what exactly is a Vehi-CROSS when it's out on the road? Well, it's different and to Isuzu a vitally important pointer to their future. Having recently abandoned production of passenger vehicles, they have decided to concentrate on their strengths, principally four wheel drive. Satomi Maruyama, Chief Designer/Manager at the European office in Brussels is on hand to point out that "passenger vehicles, are not just saloon cars you know." Of course, he is correct, the RV market in the United States is huge and Europe have been bitten by the 4 x 4 bug in a big way over the last few years. The trouble is, that since the Range Rover re-wrote the rule book in 1970, there have been no breakthroughs in off roader design. Most come across as boxy comprises, dynamically neither a proper on, or off road vehicle, whilst stylistically they are undistinguished Tonka Toy clones. Isuzu aims to change all that with what is the most visually arresting Isuzu that you have ever seen.

Maruyama produces a fax that has probably got TOP SECRET written in Japanese across the top and translates the Vehi-CROSS objectives to me. "Lightweight, compact, ecologically clean and functional. We want to produce an emotional RV, one that you will care about, not a box. For us, the design is paramount." That is good, patriotic news, because Assistant Chief Designer on this show car project is Simon Cox.

Cox, 34, from Warwickshire is best known for his design of the Lotus Elan interior. For the last three years he has been at Isuzu, "I admit that this is not the most obviously glamorous company to work for, he believes that RV, one that you will care about, not a box. For us, the design is paramount."

Front and rear views would lead you to believe that a Vauxhall Corsa had driven off the top deck of a multistory car park and landed Dunlops down onto a stationary Isuzu Trooper. In fact, that's not too far off the truth. According to Cox, "What we wanted to do was merge a saloon car with an off-roader., emphasising both the strength of a 4 x 4 and the comfort and performance of a sports car.

Maruyama, Cox, Joji Yanaka, Andrew Hill and Nick Robinson, to name the full design team, have interpreted the original brief: lightweight, but tough, environmentally friendly, to perfection. Which is how you get the name Vehi-CROSS. Say the name fast and often enough, V-e-h-i-cross - V-e-h-i-cross and it sounds as though you are hyperventilating. Cox admits it is an odd name and specifically designed the graphic with a dominant V, so that it could be abbreviated to the more macho and obviously more marketable, V-CROSS. But I doubt that many people will be too bothered by the monicker. You get the impression that if it was parked in a showroom right now, there would be queues around the block, not just to browse, but to buy. For Maruyama, "The design is crucial to the success of the Vehi-CROSS. We could only do something 1 in Europe, or possibly America. People here are less constrained and come up with concepts that are much freer. It also like this in Europe, or possibly America. People here are less constrained and come up with concepts that are much freer. It also helps that this is purely a show car, so there is much less interference from head office in Japan."

The Vehi-CROSS sits on thin, especially by current 4 x 4 standards, 205 section tyres. That's one of the environmental considerations, because you don't need two foot wide mud pluggers to play in the dirt. As most serious off roaders and Land Rover owners know, you get much better comfort and performance on sports car skinnies, as well as flattening much less flora and fauna in the process. However, the tyres do not look out of place, amply filling the four corners of the vehicle. The wide track, high ride height and minimum of overhang means that this is intended to be a serious off-roader. A bulging midriff finished in a contrasting grey to the bodywork's silver, emphasises this point. It divides the off-road hardware bolts secure the sections into position and it is time to ask Simon Cox whether this is a motor show short-cut, or a design feature.

"The aim has always been to highlight the lightweight qualities of the vehicle without detracting from it's inherent strength. So I have taken my design cues from a number of sources which include the original 2CV."

At the front is a matt black cheese grater grille made out of the high tech material, topped off by a carbon fibre dummy bonnet that has two chrome hinges and resembles an early '60s kit car. It is in fact a deliberate attempt by Cox and the team to include purely functional items. But in this case, the black panel is recessed into the bonnet which hinges forward. Carbon fibre though, constitutes the floor panels and fuel tank that lives beneath the rear seats. "We wanted to make a feature of this material, not cover it up with carpet. It is a functional and very usable, so why hide it?" asks Cox. What they do cover up though, is the spare wheel. The tailgate is a neat and very clever affair. The tailgate swings up to reveal an enclosed carrier for the spare, which itself swings outwards to reveal a conveniently low sill. "The spare wheel bulge, is a definitive RV reference point. People expect it to be somewhere, whether on the bonnet, roof or rear door. By building it into the tailgate, it looks neat, stays clean and can't be stolen." Maruyama pats the carrier proudly, before carefully shutting the tailgate. Certainly the 2CV clues are there, the corrugated panels on the doors, roof and rear door. As for the aircraft connections, apart from the exposed Allen bolts that follow the joins, there are thick, ribbed mouldings like front and rear sump guards and there is the use of carbon fibre.

What with those cheeky Corsa lights, pert wheel bulge and caressable ribs, topped off with a slim roof spoiler, this it is a definite candidate for rear of the year. In fact, the response from Mr. and Mrs. Public when the Vehi-CROSS did break cover to negotiate the private Highland roads was extremely favourable. It didn't frighten anyone outside of the target market, old folks found it cute, the very young stared open mouthed and everyone else wanted to know what it was and where they could buy it. Only an insane woman at the Ben Lawes visitor centre thought it looked like Bubble car on steroids and certainly would not part-ex her Subaru for one. I rest my case. So the Vehi-CROSS clearly cuts the visual mustard, but will it cut a dash on the closed rough roads at Glen Etive?

Well it should. After all, this stunning vehicle sits on a new, all aluminium chassis that was built by the engineering department in Japan. The long travel suspension set-up features double wishbones and twin shock absorbers. The idea is to keep the chassis light, so it weighs just 90 kg as opposed to the 145 kg of most RVs, and to be compact, which means 215 cm, as opposed to a 320 cm long. So this is no hurried, Trooper lash up, even though it has taken just ten months to get from the drawing board to road. In between times, Maruyama and Cox have been heavily involved with it's high riding spidery gait which reminds you of something distinctly Paris-Dakar. By comparison, current 4 x 4s when they are on the move look lumbering, inept and rather old fashioned.

Finally it's time to get on board to find out whether the interior lives up to he new Frontera which makes the Vehi-CROSS a very impressive part-time project. Helping to put it all together was a Birmingham based British company called Futura, who worked closely with Isuzu to make the concept work. The only noticeable compromise is the power plant. When it goes on show in Tokyo there will be a very advanced 1.6, direct injection unit under the bonnet, a close relative of the Elan engine. At the moment, there is a more humble 1.4i doing the donkey work. "I don't think anyone realised how far we were going with this vehicle" says Cox, "otherwise we'd have got hold of an Elan engine much earlier".

Nevertheless that little engine does well during the day. An exhaust box is missing and it rasps like an air cooled Beetle. On the sweeping, rough roads around Glen Etive, where only Forestry Commission Sherpa pick-ups go about their business, you first hear the distinctive sound of the Vehi-CROSS. Then it suddenly pops up over the brow of a hill, it resembles one of those vehicles which periodically emerged from Thunderbird 2's, portable Nissen hut to scout an alien landscape.

Again, the lightweight theme dictates the layout and structure of the cabin. Corrugation, which symbolises both strength and lightness are repeating moulded motifs on the instrument binnacle, door panels, transmission tunnel and fascia. And what was the inspiration for all this? "I envisaged the keel of a boat" says Cox. "It's strong and simply constructed and I wanted the corrugated beams surrounding the whole interior environment to emphasise the solidity of construction." That actually results in a pleasingly simple and logical layout. Balanced above the steering wheel is a motorcycle type binnacle. Then the 'keel' section which forms a T between the dashboard and centre console houses straightforward rotary heater controls, a radio and a button that activates a Sony Satellite navigation system. Press it and up flips an LED monitor from the corrugated panel in front of the windscreen. There is a toggle switch on the console which allows you in a Nintendoish way to plot and trace your route. But as it is programmed for a backwoods section of Japan it is not too much use in Ben Lawers. However, as the roof section pops out in simple targa fashion, there is always the option of navigating by the stars. But in order to blast along the single track road, all we need to rely on are the two small, but bright Stanley headlamps.

The view from the cockpit is excellent. As with all off road roaders, you sit high, but the huge, steeply raked windscreen frames the stunning scenery like a high definition, wide screen, TV. The view to the rear is impeded by a thick C-pillar and high bodyline, but the fixed windows and flat, immobile, door mirrors of the show car don't really help matters. The bucket seats hold you comfortably in place, and it is hard to believe this is the interior of a 4 x 4 with pattern blue inserts and minimalist dashboard. Simon

Cox apologises for the lack of sound deadening, the suspension which is set up for motor show display purposes and the fact that the whole package is much heavier than it would be in production. "If there had been more time and money, the body would have been made from alloy rather than GRP.

However, it moves in a very sprightly fashion, as the 1.4 unit works hard and the clutch, after a very hard days driving, starts to cook. Show cars are not supposed to behave like this. Sure, they can pose for the fashion still shots, but this one is behaving as though it is up for a chariot role in Ben Hur. Of course we can't go in for any off-road adventures, but at the end of the run we have to negotiate Road closed sign. That necessitates one wheel dipping into the rough stuff. Apart from the vehicle deviating a few degrees from true, I hardly notice the manoeuvre.

As we step down, the people from Futura gather round to put the Vehi-CROSS safely away in the covered trailer. I ask why Isuzu have gone to all this trouble?

"For too long", says Cox, "the Vitara has had all the attention. The original concept for the Vehi-CROSS was an off-road raider but it has since evolved to become this lightweight, sports based on-road, off-roader."

So when is it coming out Mr. Maruyama? The affable designer, just smiles enigmatically and refuses to be drawn on future production plans. He admits that something similar must be under consideration. And then there is that all-new 1.6 direct injection engine. Hardly likely to be powering future Troopers, but something a little smaller, or unusual perhaps? Other clues emerge during the day as I discover that the perhaps? Other clues emerge during the day as I discover that the door handles have been tooled especially for the Vehi-CROSS. Also, for a company like Isuzu which no longer make conventional passenger cars, an RV is the most logical 'world vehicle' which fits easily into all the important markets, particularly the United States and Europe.

Which leaves us to examine all the available evidence. and reach a hopelessly ill-informed conclusion. Firstly there's that fully, functioning lightweight chassis from Japan, which even has a proper tow hitch fitted. Now that seems like a lot of trouble to go to for a show car.In two years time, something very like the Vehi-CROSS could very be tempting you into an Isuzu showroom. We have seen and driven the future of fun 4x4s and it definitely works.

Vehi-CROSS Epilogue...

Here was a concept which was actually made from 1997 to 1999 for the Japanese market and from 1999-2001 for the American one. It shared most components with the Trooper, including both its 3.2 and 3.5 V6 engine. It also featured the TOD (Torque on Demand) 4-wheel Drive system produced by BorgWarner. Sales were intentionally limited, with only 4,309 being produced between 1999 and 2001

It was intended to showcase Isuzu's off-road technology, exemplified by the monotube shocks with external heat-expansion chambers.The Vehi-CROSS came equipped with 16" polished wheels in 1999 and 18" chrome wheels during the remainder of production.

The Vehi-CROSS combined a computer-controlled all-wheel-drive system for on-road driving and a locked-differential low gear four-wheel-drive system for off-road driving. Its computer controlled "Torque on Demand" system, with 12 independent sensors detecting wheel spin and redirecting power to the wheels with the most traction, gives the Vehi-CROSS a high level of traction on wet and icy roads. It also has a high level of performance for its height.

It was quite handy when used in action and won its class in the1998 Paris-Dakar Rally and the 1999 Australian

Safari Rally.

The thing is, the Vehi-CROSS still looks like the future. It could go on sale tomorrow This is what Autofutropolis looks like.

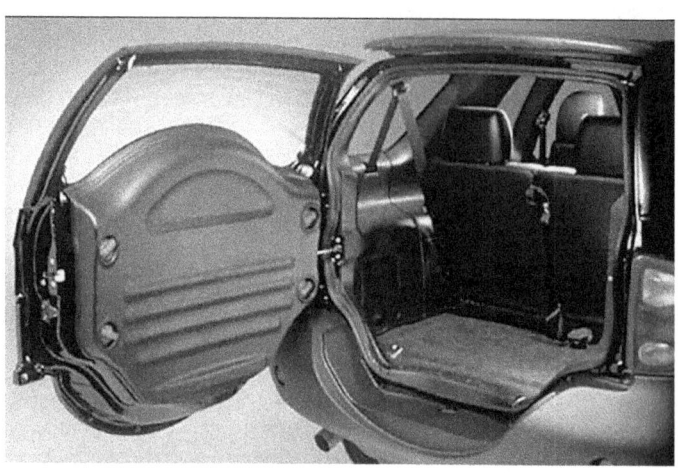

James Ruppert Is under the delusion that he can time travel. Having said that, he lives mostly in 1979 with no direct access to the modern world except through the medium of Telex and a telephone landline. Always interested in motoring history (grade 1 CSE), he bought all sorts of MOT borderline Bangers that were prehistorically awful. Once sold cars then switched to writing about used ones. Spent many years driving around the country looking at car lots and talking to blokes who sold them. Wrote for newspapers including The Independent, The Sunday Times and Evening Standard. Best known as a writer for Car magazine, Autocar, Performance Car, Supercar Classics and many others. Dreamt up the word Bangernomics in 1990 and wrote a story about buying and running an £80 Eastern Block Banger. Book of the word came out in 1993 and has found that banging on about marginal motoring only makes a marginal living. Please consider the following titles for inclusion on your bookshelves to help pay for food, fuel and automotive tat.

Order Books from www.bangernomics.com

There might also be T-Shirts and maybe other branded goods available with quite possibly some wonderful colour images from this book.

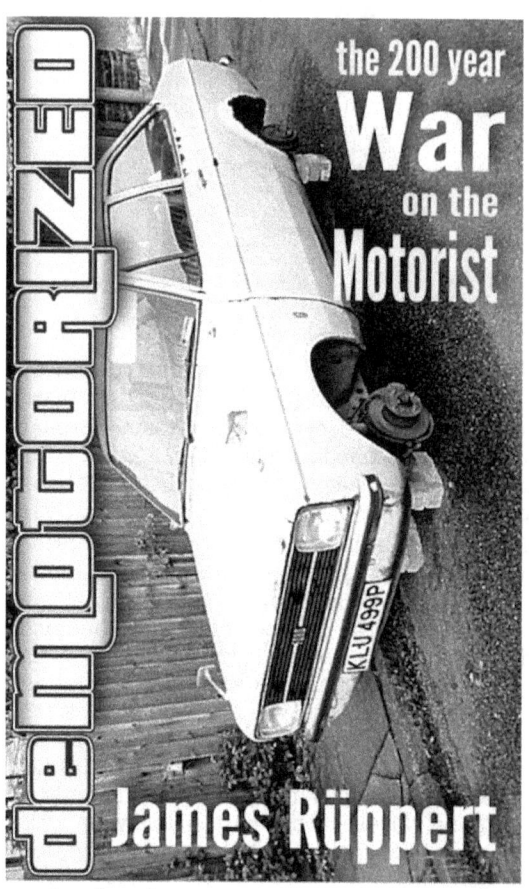

Demotorized. This is the not quite definitive history of how parking became an industry, governments overtaxed motorists, carmakers lied about how safe and environmentally friendly they were and tested their emissions on monkeys and humans. Also why robot cars are so dangerous and electric cars are not the answer. Also, who is behind the ongoing plan to Demotorize the world. Printed in 2020 it predicted the future with terrifying accuracy.
Buy it before it gets banned.

The Award Winning and so good the BBC based a documentary (Das Auto) on it **The German Car Industry, My Part in its Victory**. Winner of the Mercedes-Benz Montagu of Beaulieu Trophy for the best motoring book of year. Contains Yuppies, BMW 3, 5, 6 & 7-Series (yes that's all there was back then) and references to contemporary 1980s music.

The Critically acclaimed and best selling **The British Car Industry Our Part in Its Downfall**, which has been described as "Beautifully written with considerable wit" by the Daily Telegraph and The Daily Express said, "It's informative, well-written and extremely funny" which was really nice of them. The story of the motor industry from 1945 to 2005, explaining just why you can't buy a British built family hatchback from a British owned company. Plus all the cars, James's Dad bought.

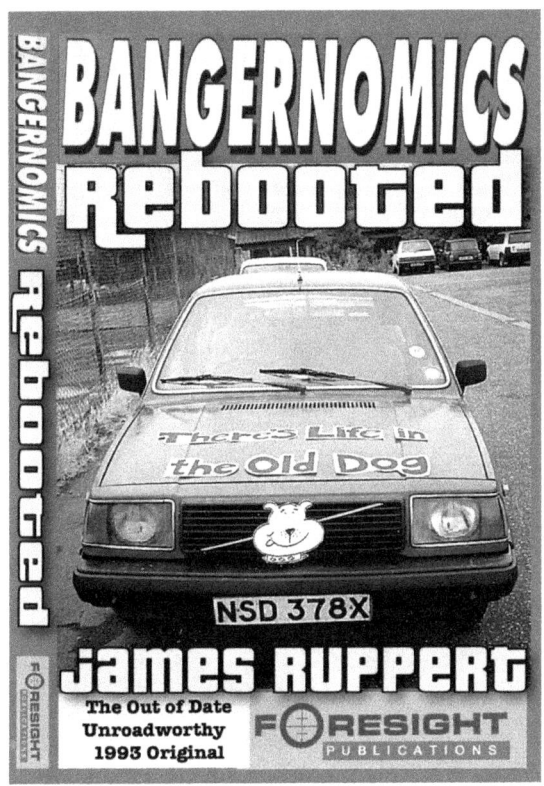

In the beginning, 1993, there was Bangernomics and now there is **Bangernomics Rebooted** which contrasts the absurd expense of buying a new car with the supreme good sense of buying well used. At a stroke depreciation no longer became an issue, running costs were slashed and there were no finance charges to be endured. Here is the original book, republished and effectively rebooted. So it is absolutely useless to any car buyer unless they have access to a time machine.

There is a new version of the **Bangernomics Bible** coming soon. Not at all sure what the format will actually be. Could be a romantic novel, a pop up might be a lot of bother, maybe a colouring one would be appreciated. Anyway working on it right now...Actually it will be the top 200 Bangernomic tipsmaybe more maybe less...

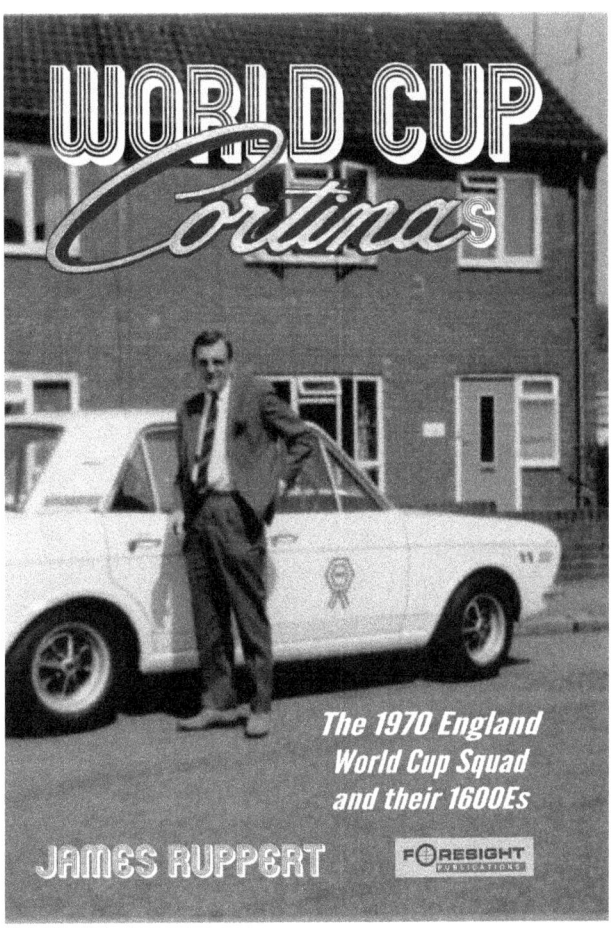

World Cup Cortinas In 1970 something very remarkable happened. Not only had England qualified for the World Cup in Mexico because they were defending champions, but most important of all Ford had loaned every squad member the greatest saloon car in the world. A book about what happened to those Ford Cortinas and how footballers bought better cars when they earned more money and no longer owned the same motors that your mum and dad drove.

Channeling the absurdist spirit of Spike Milligan" said Classic Car, others just called it "Witty", that's **My Mini Cooper Its Part in My Breakdown** which has the full history of the world's favourite small car, plus the history of what came before but not after. Also details the on-off restoration of a Mini Cooper that cost £200 in 1979. The expense of restoring the bodywork and mechanicals ought to put off most sane people. Except that original minis are always worth far more than you could imagine.

Buy real books, digital ones and T-shirts at
www.bangernomics.com

Ruppert's Bangerpedia deals with the confusing line up of noughties models. The Bangerpedia does this with a fairly ridiculous rating system involving Slog the Bangernomic Dog. The briefest of guides to each of the 700+ models includes some fairly marginal buying advice, a sarcastic appraisal and an almost definitive indication as to whether it will fit into a garage, or not.

AutoFutropolis – Car History Rebooted

Ruppert's Bangerpedia Modern Classic covers the epic '90s decade which was a golden period for Bangers. The Bangerpedia does this with a fairly ridiculous rating system involving Slog the Bangernomic Dog. The briefest of guides to each of the 528+ models includes some fairly marginal buying advice, a sarcastic appraisal and an almost definitive indication as to whether it will fit into your garage, or not.

The world of motoring is in a desperate crisis. Demonised, despised and attacked from every wrong thinking government, local authority, pressure group and even car manufacturers themselves. Bangernomics is here to bring motoring back to the masses, saving time, money and automotive headaches. Squashing together the original Bangernomics, Bangernomics Bible and Bangernomics Diet into one easily digestible guide to buying and running an older cost efficient motor. Only **Bangernomics can save the World.**

Shopping for cars can be a full time job, well it was for me anyway. In the pre Interweb age it meant actually going to look at cars for sale. It meant talking to the blokes selling the cars face to face. You learned loads lot doing it that way. With the benefit of hindsight and a time machine, some cars look cheap now, but they could well have been pretty expensive then. Find out how I got sued by one of the 'stars' of the Italian Job, was told off by the Deputy Prime Minister, find out what the worst car Sir Ian Botham ever owned was, and that time I lent my car to Bjork. Plus there are excursions around the UK that includes buying a car in Scotland and posting it to to Japan. Also looking for Bangers in Northern Ireland whilst trying to avoid the troubles. Then there is Princess Diana's Escort Ghia and the true origin of the word Bangernomics. There are Cop cars, Army surplus and even the true meaning of motoring life...

He was a man running out of time and that time was 1973. Spencer Haze is a comic superhero who first hit the 21st century in the year 2000. First on the 4Car website, then later in national newspapers and car magazines. Some say he was even on the television and might well have been real. Here is just about every frame he ever squeezed into, plus a TV script and random pictures that have never been seen before. Here is everything possibly no one ever wanted to know about a fictional bloke called Spencer who loved cars, people and the absolute truth. There are a couple of full stories, loads of articles he appeared in.

The only pro-motorist car mag in the Universe*

It costs nothing, but contains everything you need to be a more anarchistic, bolshie and less co-operative car driver.

*www.freecarmag.com

www.ingramcontent.com/pod-product-compliance
Lightning Source LLC
Chambersburg PA
CBHW061641040426
42446CB00010B/1529